Story of EDUSAT

Story of EDUSAT

Marmar Mukhopadhyay

SHIPRA

ISBN: 978-81-7541-311-5

2009 Impression
First Published in 2006

Story of Edusat

Published by:
SHIPRA PUBLICATIONS
115-A, Vikas Marg, Shakarpur, Delhi – 110092 (India)
Ph.: 91-11-65277210, 22500954 Fax: 22458662;

Branch Office: 115, Munish Plaza, 20, Ansari Road, Daryaganj, Delhi 110002; Ph. 91-11-65946453, 9810522367

Email: info@shiprapublications.com
Website: www.shiprapublications.com

Dedicated at the Lotus Feet
Swami Sachchidananda Giri
Our Revered Gurudev

Preface

It was an unusual Sunday morning gathering at the India Habitat Centre. We were just 15 people. There were retired diplomats, retired senior police officers, retired bureaucrats, retired senior personnel from the Army, Airforce and Navy, and a few who were on the queue to retire. The group was being chaired by Dr. Karan Singh, an outstanding scholar, statesman and politician. One of the members of the group asked the chairman, "what are the great programmes of your government?" The chairman referred to three programmes, namely rural employment programme, mid-day meal programme for the primary school children and SSA. He argued that if the poor people in the rural area can be guaranteed 100 days of employment in a year, children get nutritious meal at least once in a day in the school and education can be spread to cover every child in the country, country's future can be ensured.

It was a special delight for me, since I have been intensely involved at the policy level of the SSA and the mid-day meal programme of the government. When the group got busy discussing SSA and the mid-day meal programme, I mentally revisited the primary schools in the villages of Uttar Pradesh, Maharashtra, Tamil Nadu and West Bengal that I had recently visited; classes were overflowing with enthusiastic lively children with dreams in their eyes; indeed unbelievable. There were classes with 102 children in grade II and 82 in grade III. Teachers were clueless about what to do with such large number of children bubbling with enthusiasm in every class. I visited the places where mid-day meal was being cooked; I tasted the soyabean-potato curry in one of the primary schools. What a taste! I envied the children. I was brought back to the meeting by certain questions and criticisms.

What flashed through me is an excruciating pain, not from the criticisms of the schemes. That such a huge uprising within education, so much of enthusiasm of illiterate parents and their children unfolding Indian resurgence will get lost in the dins of daily chores; history will not be written. Future generations will be deprived access to the great experience of the second freedom of India. No body will know the heroes and heroines of this great social drama. The educational planners and managers at the Centre and States, captains of the well meaning NGOs, who made the difference in the lives of children and the country would get lost with time.

I feel the same pain and agony as I look back at our experience and involvement in formulation of the National Policy on Education 1986. With my involvement from the very beginning, I still connect the points of history in policy making from then till now. There are a few others who have already called it a day. We have Challenge of Education, Policy document and the Programme of Action. Nobody knows how were these done; who did all these. Nights that were spent in Shastri Bhawan and NIEPA by many of us; our youthful Prime Minister, Rajiv Gandhi waiting for the draft of the policy document in the midnight,—all lost. These are not just facts for counting; these are stories that can inspire our future generations. These events need to find places they deserve.

Story of EDUSAT is similar – a magnificent concept pregnant with rich possibilities of transforming India through education at fast pace; a unique idea anywhere in the world. I have had the rare privilege of being involved with EDUSAT ever since DECU called me up. There must have been lot of creative ideas, considerations and debates in ISRO before crystallizing the idea itself. We do not know all that. It is exciting to even imagine how creative must have been the process of conceiving the idea. Without documentation, all such great events and processes remain only a tacit knowledge beyond the reach of many. Ronald Havelock, in his monumental work, 'Communication of Innovations', lamented how such great experiences of innovations get lost due to non-documentation. I took the plunge to present the story of EDUSAT to a larger audience.

Development and Educational Communication Unit (DECU) of ISRO, was entrusted the responsibility of steering the project on dedicated satellite for education which was later christened as EDUSAT. I was associated in drafting the concept document, *Educating the Nation: Need for a Dedicated Satellite.* With modest experience, as an amateur, in developing and producing educational video programmes, the magnitude of the challenge was of great attraction. It provided an exciting opportunity to conceptualize the application and impact of a dedicated satellite with multiple transponders and channels, for education alone. It brought an important opportunity of projecting the idea of 'Educating the Nation.' Subsequently, I was called upon to hold the national consultation on EDUSAT jointly with DECU, and finally authoring the project document.

The dedicated satellite for education was launched on September 20, 2004, more than a year ago. There have been some efforts to set up the network of reception facility at the ground level which is key instrument for effective utilization of EDUSAT. However, reception network is still to be activated and utilized. Conceptualizing, designing the roadmap, and implementing such a massive complicated project of educating the nation through multiple languages is a massive challenge without parallel anywhere in the world. In such kind of project design and implementation, success and failure meet each other eye-to-eye which is nothing unusual.

I understand that sharing a story that is still unfolding is not usual in the Indian academic cultural milieu. EDUSAT being in the public domain, I do hope that this unfolding story will attract many talents to share their creative ideas into shaping the national agenda of educating the nation. I shall consider my efforts rewarded if this story generates a constructive debate on how to go about using a dedicated satellite in education that fulfils the mission of educating students in schools, colleges and universities in the formal, nonformal and open and distance education systems, educating people of all ages for lifelong learning, and educating people in a variety of careers for continuing education.

This treatise is essentially the outcome of my association in different stages of development of EDUSAT; in the process I had to consult a large number of people from different walks of life. All of them are part of the story, some belong to the known some to the unknown. I am grateful to all of them. Although not directly related to the authoring of this book, my most honest gratitude is to Sri B.S. Bhatia, Director DECU. Without his invitation right at the stage of conceptualization, I would have been an onlooker to this important development in the history of our nation. I thank Sri D. Kumar of Shipra Publications for undertaking the publication of this book.

14 November, 2005 **Marmar Mukhopadhyay**
New Delhi

Contents

1

Before EDUSAT

Rationale

India faces the twin challenge of providing quality of life for her people and be competitive in a globalized world. These are interrelated and interdependent. Without an educated populace, India will not be able to be competitive in the global arena. Hence, an educated India is an imperative for her to be competitive. Also, a literate and educated world community is the only guarantee for a prosperous, peaceful and happy world living in harmony. The E-9 conference in New Delhi in 1993 declared education as the only defence of the country. It is not without reasons that beginning with the Jomtien conference in 1990, the world came together in order to create an educated and ever learning world. This was again reiterated in the Dakar conference in 2001. The spirit of an educated and continuously learning world was the central theme of the report to the UNESCO by the International Commission on Education for the 21st Century—*Learning: the Treasure Within*. For India the challenge is educating one billion people, the number that is growing every year.

It is no doubt a big challenge. If it appears to be a utopia; it is a 'necessary utopia'. The challenge, of course, is very complicated because of India's multicultural, multi-religious, multi-linguistic composition within a multiparty democratic polity. The issue of educating the nation is equally complicated because of regional diversity and disparity, and gender inequality in education. Educating such a complex fusion of a nation can be accomplished in addition to organized conventional educational institutions by well planned and well executed adjunct initiatives.

Previous Efforts

EDUSAT is not the first and maiden effort in pressing satellite in Indian education. The history of satellite in education spans over more than four decades. There have been several landmark experiments with satellite in education including interactive instruction. Satellite began to play its role in Indian education with the introduction of educational television in 1961-62. Nonetheless, Indian landmark in satellite in education is considered to be the Satellite Instructional Television Experiment (SITE) in 1971. There is some sense of pride about SITE experiment as it never misses a mention even after 34 years; Dr. Kasturirangan mentioned SITE in his G Ram Reddy memorial lecture in IGNOU in 2004 (text of his address can be seen in ISRO website) with lot of fondness. I shall not get into the details of SITE here since this has been dealt with elaborately by Dr. Parhar in her book, *Satellite in Education*.

Meanwhile, Asian Games in 1982 revolutionized Indian television, and its impact was perceptible in educational television as well when programmes graduated from black and white to colour. National Policy on Education (NPE 1986) provided fresh impetus to the use of educational television. NPE 1986 provided a special thrust through a centrally sponsored scheme on educational technology. Close on the heels came the Indo-US sub-commission project Classroom 2000+ in 1989-90 on experimenting with interactive learning through satellite delivered education with interaction through keypads at the learning ends by CIET. Details are given by Dr. Parhar's book, *Satellite in Education*. We had the privilege of evaluating the experiment.

ISRO with its innovative and creative vision has looked at the possibility and utility of satellite in education and other service sectors. It pioneered experiments in interactive learning through satellite by allowing and encouraging use of the left over life of INSAT series 2 for educational experiments by setting up the Training and Development Communication Channel (TDCC). ISRO parked one of its mobile uplink stations atop a truck at IGNOU in early 1990s. Several interesting experiments were conducted with the TDCC. Many of the educational institutions started using TDCC channel either from Ahmedabad or IGNOU campus in New Delhi for delivering interactive instructions through one-way video and two way audio. DECU itself offered two-way video-interactive programme on educational media for international participants. Besides, IGNOU, NIEPA, NCERT, NIOS, AIMA, IITD etc. used this facility.

The TDCC experience led to another major innovation – launching of DEP-DPEP for in-service education of teachers through distance education under DPEP. It was decided to equip all DIETs with DRS facilities for receiving lessons delivered through TDCC.

Slowly but steadily, the voice for a dedicated channel for education was gaining ground. By mid 1990s, a committee comprising heads of major national institutions was already involved in shaping the concept of a dedicated channel for education. Gyan Darshan and Gyan Vani are the dedicated television and radio channels in education. The TDCC experience on one hand and demand for a dedicated channel for education on the other got a boost from an unusual quarter. UNESCO initiated the process of developing national action plan for in-service education of primary teachers through satellite supported distance education in the Asian region countries.

National Action Plan: In-Service Education of Primary Teachers

Following the E-9 summit in New Delhi in 1993, UNESCO regional office in Bangkok mobilized resources from the Asian Development Bank for the five Asian large population countries, namely Bangladesh, China, India, Indonesia, and Pakistan to develop National Action Plan for in-service education of primary school teachers through distance education. Unlike the other four countries, Government of India transferred the funds to UNESCO in New Delhi and assigned the responsibility of developing the National Action Plan. I had the privilege of being called upon as consultant to UNESCO for drafting The National Action Plan under the overall guidance of a steering committee headed by Vice-Chancellor, IGNOU.

In developing the National Action Plan, there were extensive consultations with over 350 educational personnel belonging to a variety of backgrounds namely primary teachers, teacher educators, and educational researchers, planners and administrators, experts in educational technology and educationists. The respondents to such discussions were selected from all over the country.

National Action Plan proposed to set up a four-tier Indian Training and Education Network for Development (INTEND), these tiers being national, regional, state, district (and block) levels. Main contention was to connect all the DIETs and all the block level resource centres, providing an opportunity for creating a countrywide virtual classroom with the feasibility and flexibility of generating state specific virtual classrooms as well as virtual classrooms at the regional level. Since it was to focus on primary education, the SCERT at the state level was visualized to be the nodal centres; the DIETs and PTTIs were proposed to be the main delivery institutions.

Virtual classrooms were visualized to be created through two-way videoconferencing using either one of the transponders in the existing satellite or using the fibre-optic network making full use of the expanding PSTN and ISDN networks. To support the in-service education of primary teachers, the need for software was recognized. As a part of the project development, an inventory of educational software available for primary teacher education was developed. The project also considered various issues like manpower requirement, capacity building, information systems development, role of national, state and district levels institutions, role of other departments, phasing, and monitoring and supervision.

The project was estimated to cost Rs 127 million during the ninth plan, and Rs 187 million during the 10th plan with a total annual training output of 8.1 3 million teachers.

The document proposed phasing out of the programme so that requisite funds could be mobilized over a period of time. Initially, it was decided to implement the National Action Plan in Gujarat and Madhya Pradesh. This would have given an opportunity to experiment in two different languages.

The project was taken up at the Government of India, Ministry of Human Resource Development. There have been several meetings and discussions. However, the project seems to have lost its way.

State Initiatives

While majority of all these innovative efforts and thinking were going on at the national level, certain silent but massive transformation was happening at the state level. Encouraged by TDCC activities, Goa University set up its own interactive network connecting all its affiliated colleges; DECU, Ahmedabad was used as delivery hub. Gujarat set up a massive interactive communication network on its own through fibre-optic cable network connecting all the districts and blocks with the hub at Gandhinagar. Madhya Pradesh set up an uplink station at Bhopal in the Academy of Administration, and downlink facilities in every district at the DIETs. Karnataka set up a network with a smart uplink facility loaded on a jeep-top and downlink facilities in all the districts. Orissa also had similar facilities. All these state networks were set up and activated much before EDUSAT was launched or even documented.

Conclusion

It would be evident that EDUSAT is the culmination of years of micro and meso-level experiments in satellite delivered interactive learning. The brief account submitted above provides a glimpse of different but important trends of development. First is the steady shift from broadcast to interactive instruction. Then is the enlargement in the scope of experiments; and third is the growing state initiative in satellite based interactive instruction for education and other domains of development.

2

Conceptualizing EDUSAT

Introduction

Sri Bhatia called me up from Ahmedabad asking for an opportunity to get together to discuss the idea of a dedicated satellite for education. I welcomed the idea, and invited him and his colleagues to NIEPA, New Delhi. During the first discussion, I also invited a few other scholars from a few other national institutions. The discussion was rich and productive. Having been personally associated with similar tasks earlier, I was conscious of the complexity of transforming the idea into a document. Immediately after the discussion, I asked Bhatia whether there is someone who could document this concept and provide a conceptual framework for an educational satellite. Bhatia called upon me to offer the first conceptual document. A God sent opportunity; I accepted the invitation to draft the document. Having dabbled in making educational video films and researching in media and educational technology myself for long, I knew in my heart that the conventional education sector will not be able to make use of such a massive facility. A dedicated satellite will throw up an opportunity to educate our countrymen and women from all walks of life. I, therefore, oriented the document, '*Educating the Nation*' Indeed, educating one and all of the one billion plus Indians.

The first draft of the conceptual document that I titled, '*Educating the Nation: Need for a Dedicated Satellite*' was presented to a group of experts comprising scientists, technologists and a few former space scientist from ISRO in Pune. The draft was reviewed, commented upon, appreciated with some important suggestions for improvement and modification. Accordingly, I modified the first draft and submitted to DECU, in Ahmedabad. At this stage, the document contained rationale for dedicated satellite, channel count and proposal for their allocation to different fields, network description, software, management structure, etc. There was no reference to the satellite configuration, teaching end hubs and learning end reception centres. The document was then enriched with the configuration of the satellite, teaching centre hubs, and learning centers with RoT and SIT definitions developed by the scientists in ISRO[1]. This document is dated July 2002.

The 35 page document published originally by DECU, and republished by NIEPA later, was organized around the challenge of educating a nation—adult literacy, school education, higher and professional education, massive gap between the targets and achievements so far, response to the challenge, policies, programmes and ground realities, facilities on ground, content development, educational software, and management—cost and budgeting, coordination and collaboration and management structure.

The Challenge

The document contains elaborate details of developments in

various levels of education since independence with tables, charts and graphs. This brings into focus the spectacular expansion, diversification and developments in education since independence, with yet a massive gap in fulfilling national obligations in education. The innovative aspect was highlighting the challenge of creating the Knowledge Society that requires educating the nation on a continuing basis. 'Educating the Nation' requires educating everyone in the nation within and outside the school. 'In practical terms, education has to be provided in curricular as well as in other areas. Should we accept this new paradigm of human development, it offers us a three-dimensional challenge of education for all ages, education of in and out-of-school people, and education in various occupations (Figure 2.1).

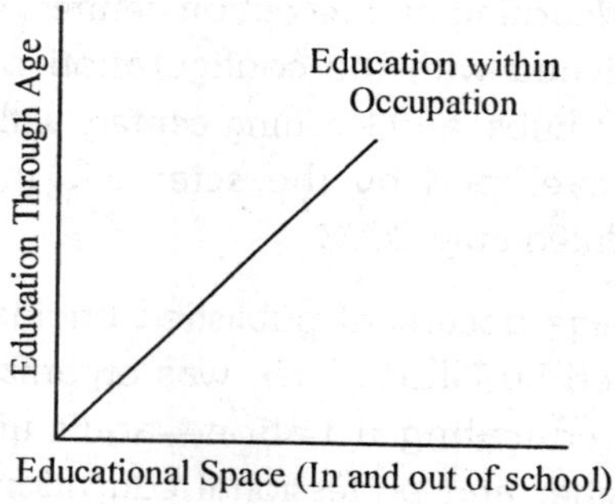

Fig. 2.1: Three-dimensional challenge of Educating the Nation

Since the challenge is multifarious, colossal and complex, simple and routine response will be grossly inadequate. Search for a possible solution must venture into the domains so far unknown. Developments in technology, particularly in computers, television, Internet, telephone, satellite, fiber-optic cabling, etc. provide significant and meaningful instruments to respond to this challenge. Over the years, Indian scientists and technologists have developed considerable mastery over such technological tools, and India has emerged as a major software and leading satellite producing country with capabilities of launching its own satellites. The document enlisted the following avenues:

- One way TV broadcast
- Interactive TV via phone in
- Interactive TV through computer support through e-mail,
- Video conferencing
- Computer conferencing
- Telephone conferencing
- Web-based instruction etc.

Bhatia wrote in his foreword to the document, "The educational institutions of the country have continuously endeavoured to use the latest technology to support the process of education. The Education Ministry was amongst the first to support and join the satellite instructional television experiment way back in 1975 and it subsequently set up the central and state institutes of educational technologies to use satellite television for primary education. The UGC through its Consortium of Educational Communication and EMRC-AVRCs actively utilize satellite broadcasting for higher education. The IGNOU too has used satellite broadcasting now leading to the operationalisation of the Gyan Darshan and Gyan Vani channels".

The document contended that separate dedicated channels are required to service the educational needs of different groups of learners in different languages. Accordingly, a channel count was developed (Table 1).

Educational Channels

As mentioned earlier, the number of educational channels had to be decided on the basis of careful need analysis in order to provide education through 16 different regional languages. Adopting a wide range of interactive techniques, the minimum number of channels was worked out to be 72. However, ISRO had maintained all along that number of channels will not be a constraining factor. Original proposal of 72 channels were:

Table 1: The Channel Count

Content	*Remarks*	*No of Channels*
School education	One dedicated channel per state	28
Higher and professional education	One dedicated channel per state	28
Science and technology for all	Hindi and English (e.g. Discovery/National Geographic)	02
Language learning	Indian and foreign languages	01
Youth Channel	Education in sports, music, dramatics, etc	02
Executive and career development	Continuing education of workforce-Hindi and English	02
Gold Channel	For senior citizens-Hindi and English	02
Women's development	Hindi and English	02
Heritage	Education in Indian scriptures and culture	01
Toddler's Channel	Cartoon network type	02
Health	Hindi and English	02
Total		72

The original Channel Count considered reaching out to every kind of citizens in the country with the basic spirit of educating the nation. Another important feature was creating provision for delivery of non-formal education through Hindi and English. Although this was not ideal, this was the most feasible option given the large number of languages in which the people of India speak. The other important feature was provision of state channels separately for school education, and higher and professional education. It is only through such dedicated state channels that it will be possible to deliver education through the regional languages.

Technology Configuration[2]

There are two components of the technology configuration, namely the space segment and the ground segment. The requirement of the space segment is necessarily based on need assessment. The initial analysis indicated a requirement of 72 channels and additional eight channels for further expansion over 10 years and 14 transponders. Accordingly, the configuration of the proposed satellite was:

Three satellites each of

- KU band
    1. to meet the former educational needs
    2. 4 regional beam, EIRP = 54dBw, G/T = 8dB/K
    3. to meet nonformal educational needs
    4. 1 India beam EIRP 49dBw, G/T = 3dB/K
- Extended C band
    1. 1 national beam with 6 transponders
    2. EIRP 37dBw, G/T-5dB/K

3. to support existing INSAT educational requirements

The first satellite can be GSAT 3. The other two satellites can be with onboard regeneration and multiplexing facilities like

- 4dB advantage due to no back off goes to better availability
- smaller uplink station due to link isolation, and
- facing out of extended she band to accommodate OBP payload

The visual is reproduced below:

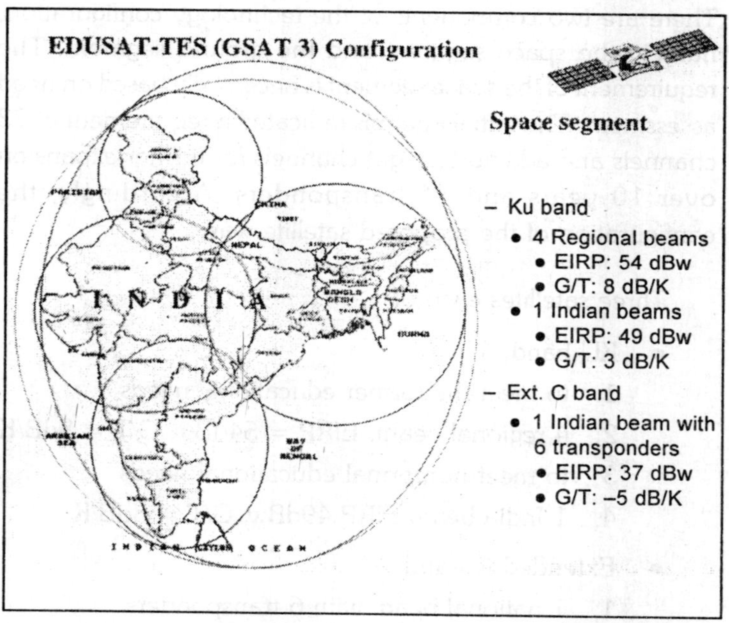

Fig. 2.2: EDUSAT 1 (GSAT 3) Configuration

The space segment needed to be corroborated with programmes and infrastructure support at the ground level. The ground segment component was proposed to comprise:

- use of DVB-RCS open standard in KU band
- small two-way interactive remote stations at district levels
- DRS at remote stations with WLL and repeater attached for talkback

In terms of geographical locations, ideally ground segment will require:

- server and studio at state level
- ROT at all primary and upper primary schools,
- SIT at all DIETs and BRCs (Block Resource Centre),
- SIT at all secondary and senior secondary schools,
- SIT+ROT+CORDECT at all colleges and universities,
- ROT+CORDECT at all gram panchayats:

The document also made a detailed assessment of facilities on ground, primarily flagging the NIC network connecting all districts, expanding computer facilities in schools, colleges and universities, the DRS installations for interactive teleconferencing in DIETs, IGNOU Regional Centres and several other networks, expanding outreach of PSTN and ISDN telephone networks throughout the country.

Content Development and Software

The problem of content development changes with the scope of education within the 3-D paradigm. For conventional school, and higher and professional education, curriculum is well defined by the respective state boards of school education and the universities; so are the cases with open schools and open universities. There is a fresh and daunting challenge in unconventional areas like education through ages, and education in careers.

There are networks of educational technology and communication institutions, like CIET-SIETs, AVRC-EMRCs, TTTIs, CETs in IITs, IGNOU, NIOS that produce educational software. Despite the debate between software for content orientation versus enrichment education, software have been developed covering content areas. The major issue is the quality of software. There are several generations of technology used in developing such educational software and archiving such software is not beyond question. What is needed is developing a comprehensive information system, evaluating quality and usability and archiving them.

Main pedagogical thrust in satellite based education is on interactive videoconferencing. The idea is: selected excellent teachers shall teach the subjects from the teaching end studio which can be received at the different learning ends. The learners will have access to the teacher for asking questions, making observations and comments through the satellites. This will create a virtual classroom – state classrooms for state channels and national classrooms for national channels. Such live instructional sessions can be recorded, digitized and archived for reuse and retrieval at will.

Organization and Management

The conceptualization of the technology configuration, Channel Count in the given backdrop of multilingual society that India is, organization and management of satellite based education pose a serious challenge. Without active and significant involvement of the states, there will be very little opportunity of making much headway in translating the magnificent concept of EDUSAT. Accordingly, it was proposed to set up a Satellite Based Educational and Instructional Technology Authority (SEITA) to provide direction and manage EDUSAT. The proposed configuration is reproduced below:

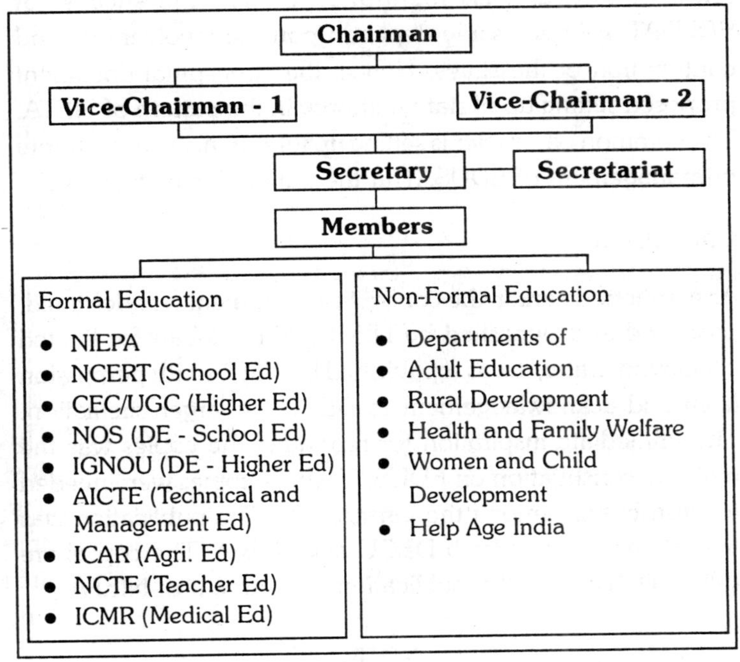

Fig. 2.3: SEITA Composition
(Setellite-based Educational and Instructional Technology Authority)
alternativle title: Setellite-based Educational
Television Authority (SETA)

The proposal is to have a full-time secretary to assist the authority. As a general pattern, it is visualized that the Department of Space will look after the space segment whereas the Ministry of Human Resource Development will be responsible for the ground segment; Ministry of Information Technology can be involved in management of IT component of the ground segment; the member institutions will be responsible for content development and development of relevant software. As mentioned earlier, the success of EDUSAT will necessarily depend upon the involvement and contribution of the states. Hence, the conceptual document proposed setting up of state authority in the pattern of SIETA. The common parameter is setting up inter-ministerial authority of management of EDUSAT at the national and state levels.

Conclusion

As mentioned earlier, the conceptual document was designed, produced and published by DECU, Ahmedabad for limited circulation. Later, it was republished by NIEPA with permission from and acknowledgement to DECU for larger circulation. The immediate inspiration for reprinting the copies was the national consultation on EDUSAT where copies were needed for distribution among the participants. The publication was free of charge from both DECU and NIEPA. The copies are still available from the publication department of NIEPA.

NOTES

1. Thanks to Bhatia and DECU, credit for authorship was given to me with acknowledgement of contributions made by ISRO scientists.
2. Quoted from the original concept document, *Educating the Nation: Need for a Dedicated Satellite.*

3

Developments So Far

Introduction

The concept life of EDUSAT is about four years, the conceptual document itself has lived a life of more than three years. Counting from the day of launching of the satellite, 20 September 2004, the satellite will complete one year on the September 20th, 2005. Leaving aside about six weeks for placing the satellite into the geosynchronous orbit, satellite already had an active life of more than ten months. Considering that the life of a satellite is estimated at seven years, it has already lived one-seventh of its life. In terms of costs, estimated at Rs. 1,000 for the satellite, the nation has already spent more than Rs. 140 crores so far (September, 2005). It may be worthwhile and interesting to review the developments that have taken place since its conceptualization and the first dialogue in early 2002 between Bhatia and me.

Risking the repetition, just to remind the reader that I presented the first draft of EDUSAT, then known by the title, Educating the Nation, in Pune held on March 11, 2002. Our first meeting with Bhatia and his colleagues was held in NIEPA in January 2002.

First Presentation

One important event in the life of EDUSAT was a brilliant (power point) presentation of the concept of the dedicated satellite by Dr. Kasturirangan to the then Minister for Human Resource Development, Government of India in New Delhi. During the first presentation, all senior functionaries of the Ministry, heads of major national institutions were present. I was invited by DECU[1].

It was at this meeting that ISRO announced that the satellite would be launched by March 2005 and called upon the education sector to get ready. In author's intervention, based on my modest experience in educational media and technology, attention was drawn to the daunting tasks ahead and expressed the fear that our own education sector may fall far too short to match the time frame put out by ISRO. Unless we get into this right now, the hungry satellite may have to wait endlessly in the sky which has actually happened later (it is fourteen months, November, 2005, and the ground segments are yet to be ready).

Constitution of Committees

Government constituted committees separately for elementary and teacher education, secondary education and higher education rather unimaginatively comprising only of administrators, usually the heads of educational institutions, to examine the issues in EDUSAT and submit recommendations. Without the inputs from professionals and academicians, the committees were clueless how to go about it. The committee on elementary education met couple of times and produced a document that had very little use.

Committees on secondary and higher education met several times without any output. This was completely infructuous an exercise that took long time causing severe and irreparable damage to the timeframe of EDUSAT.

Literally, nothing happened during the next fourteen months. Shri Bhatia called me up again to share his agony; he also mentioned that ISRO has completed the design of the satellite, and it is about to move towards assembling the satellite. The bright prospect of the launching of the satellite on time, if not before hand, was rather unnerving since we had not moved much, if at all. At Bhatia's instance, I visited DECU and we decided to jointly host a national consultation on educational satellite

National Consultation on EDUSAT

National consultation on EDUSAT was held from 23rd to 25 July 2003 in NIEPA jointly by DECU and NIEPA. Dr Kasturirangan presented his concept again, in all its parameters in his inaugural address at the national consultation on 23rd July, 2003 (Appendix 2). The keynote address was delivered by Professor R H Dave, former director of UNESCO Institute of Education, Hamburg. The consultation was concluded with the valedictory address by Smt Kumud Bansal, then Union Additional Secretary (Education), Government of India. Consultation was participated by 94 senior educational administrators from the centre and state governments, academicians, instructional technologists, media specialists and space scientists. The consultations were held with 8 to 10 participants specializing in each of the following areas:

- Elementary Education,
- Secondary Education,
- Higher Education,
- Teacher Education,
- Technical Education,
- Women Education,
- Open and Distance Education, and
- Vocational Education.

Each group submitted detailed recommendations in their own respective areas. A few participants also contributed background papers to the consultation. The detailed report of the National Consultation[2] was published by NIEPA in October, 2003. Based on the discussion and recommendations in different groups, I developed a 19-point roadmap, EDUSAT: Road Ahead.

EDUSAT: Road Ahead

1. An Inter-Ministerial meeting be held, involving Departments of Education, Women and Child Development, Sports and Youth, Social Welfare, Science and Technology, Electronics, Information and Broadcasting, Labour (six different channels proposed need support of these departments).
2. Till such time, an Authority is formed, a Steering Committee be appointed with Additional Secretary as Chairperson.
3. An institute should be identified as nodal agency for the ground segment preparedness. An Advisory Committee should be constituted representing

various institutions, like IGNOU, UGC, NCERT, NIEPA, NIOS, CBSE, IIT, etc. With the advice of the Advisory Committee, the course of action should be decided by the nodal institution that will also be responsible for implementation.

4. The entire EDUSAT preparedness should be projectised. A comprehensive project should comprise DPRs on elementary education, secondary education, higher education, vocational and technical education, open and distance education, and women's education. The project document should be ready by the end of December 2003.
5. As mentioned by the Additional Secretary in her valedictory address at the National Consultation, it will be necessary to involve the states. Each state will be provided with two dedicated channels, one each for School Education and Higher and Professional Education. States have to be involved in planning, particularly for these channels, and providing ground segment facilities. Following actions are suggested:
   - (i) A meeting of the Education Secretaries dealing with School and Higher Education be convened.
   - (ii) Each State should set up Consultative Groups on Elementary Education, Secondary Education, Teacher Education, Higher Education, Vocational and Technical Education to come out with State Plans for implementing EDUSAT, particularly for using the regional language channels.
6. State governments and agencies should be encouraged and called upon to conduct state level

consultative meetings to generate necessary awareness and concern.

7. Depending upon the hours and the timing of school and collegiate education, timetable should be drafted indicating time for broadcast radio, broadcast TV, interactive radio, interactive TV, computer based virtual classrooms and time for retrieval from the software archives.
8. Such timetable can only lead to more accurate assessment of educational software requirements (For example, virtual classroom either through computer communication or interactive radio or interactive TV may not necessarily require the conventional video programmes or computer aided learning material).
9. The CEC maintains a directory of software produced by AVRCs, and EMRCs. Similar database may be available with CIET on software produced by SIET for elementary education. Except the software produced by NIOS, there may not be any educational software for the secondary education[3]. The TTTIs and IITs have produced large number of video and multi-media software for technical education. Immediate action is needed to collect information and develop a directory of educational software in various sectors with brief annotation.
10. NIOS has already taken a lead in developing educational software for secondary education. The institute should be strengthened and also asked to enhance software production to cover courses from 6th to 12th standards. Since much of the curriculum is common, it will have the facility of inter-operability and adaptation.

11. In order to fill in the void in secondary education, teacher education, vocational education, women's education, there has to be special efforts for software production.
    (i) Agencies should be identified for each one of these sectors for production of software.
    (ii) Video lectures and tutored video should be developed at the first instance. These are less expensive but equally instructive.
    (iii) Funds have to be identified and allocated for the production of software.
12. There are large number of private firms producing multi-media training and educational software. Through public advertisements, such agencies should be identified and commissioned for production of computer-based interactive learning material[4]. Incidentally, multi-media CD software is cheaper than the video format.
13. The cost of Hubs at the state level will cost approximately Rs 2.0 crores. These will be required for every state. Hence, at least Rs 70 crores will be required to create the State Hubs except in such states where the Hubs have already been created. The funds have to be made available by the Centre or the states have to create funds with multi-departmental contributions.
14. It is estimated that each reception station will cost approximately Rs 0.80 lakh[5] with return path facility to be provided at schools, colleges, teacher education institutions, etc. The total number of institutions is estimated to be about 1.40 lakhs. The estimated

expenditure for the reception stations would be Rs 1120 crores. This does not include the cost of the ROTs for the elementary schools, which is likely to cost approximately Rs 24,000 crores. Immediate attention is needed to take decision about locating funds for reception stations.

15. Evaluation of government sponsored Educational Technology Scheme as well as other research studies indicate:
    (i) Education Radio and TV are least used.
    (ii) Wherever these are used, there have been very little impact on learning
    (iii) Wherever educational media has been used with teacher intervention or animation, there is positive impact on learning.
    (iv) These experiences and evidences call for serious effort for orientation and capacity building of the users for satellite developed educational programmes.
16. For the virtual classrooms, competent and effective teachers are to be identified in each state. They need to be trained to communicate through this new media.
17. Mass teacher orientation programmes need to the launched to create awareness as well as skill in using satellite delivered education.
18. Each state should create a Resource Group for various levels of education for designing and software preparation, capacity building, monitoring and evaluation.

19. Despite tremendous potentialities, EDUSAT runs the risk of gross underutilization. It would be necessary to develop a monitoring mechanism, and conduct periodic evaluation about its functioning and impact on learning.

Projectization

This was an important watershed. Ministry of Human Resource Development started taking interest in the subject. Then Joint Secretary (School Education) was made in charge of EDUSAT. Out of the many recommendations, Joint Secretary picked up only one: 'Application of satellite in education should be projectised'.

At the instance of the Ministry of Human Resource Development, I agreed to convert the concept in a project document; Ministry of Human Resource Development provided the necessary financial support to accomplish this task. Before drafting the project document, I decided to consult experts and state officials; I was more than convinced that success of EDUSAT can be achieved only with the involvement of the states. I traveled to a few states, namely Madhya Pradesh, Karnataka, Gujarat, Orissa, West Bengal, etc. and held meetings with senior officials like principal secretaries, commissioners of education as well as academicians. In West Bengal, the experience was different. West Bengal College and University Teachers Association organized a seminar in Jadavpur University. This was addressed among others by both the ministers of school education and higher education, several university vice-chancellors, eminent educational technologists, and participated by more than 150 scholars from various universities and colleges. I had a separate meeting with heads of major state institutions like state boards of primary, secondary and higher education, Madrassa Education, State Open School, SCERT under the chairmanship of the Minister in-charge of school education. So was the experience in Madhya Pradesh where a day-long deliberation was called by the Principal Secretary Education, attended by senior state officials, academicians from various levels of education. DECU conducted many such consultative exercises primarily with its clear focus on launching pilot experiments with EDUSAT.

I also consulted many experts and educationists. Most memorable interview and discussion was with President A.P.J. Abdul Kalam, (Box 1).

Box 1. Meeting with President APJ Abdul Kalam, President of India

While drafting the project document on EDUSAT, an appointment was sought with President A P J Abdul Kalam. He granted the appointment, and I met him along with Professor Jaya Indiresan. There were two different experiences in this important meeting. One was consultation on the technical aspects of the project, particularly choice of technology, and second was the concern for education of Indian children and youth.

President Kalam appreciated the initiative of ISRO and mentioned with sense of pride about his Indian mission on space technology. He, however, advised us to look for alternative technologies also like fiber-optic cable network. His basic contention was that there is a gap between the audible sound and the lip movement, though extremely small, when communication is made through satellite based technology. Although adult learners may not be distracted, 'children are extremely sensitive and perceptive; they are likely to observe it and find fun in the lessons'. His critical and penetrating observation is admirable.

On his own, he picked up the issue of students learning through virtual classroom methodology. He advised us to package learning and ensure that the students learn their contents and subjects and are able to get scores in the examination which is extremely important for their future career[6]. As a student of instructional sciences, I was deeply impressed with his understanding of packaging learning, pragmatism, and more serious concern for the students at the end of the continuum.

It was obviously a rare privilege to meet the President of India. His humility, warmth, non-hesitant expression of concern about children of India and his confidence on India's potentiality to emerge as a developed nation was inspiring.

Another interesting experience was consultation through e-mail and Internet. I shared the idea of a dedicated satellite for education with a number of Indian diaspora-educationists, particularly in the USA. Some important ideas, suggestions, and feedback were received individually from many. This includes Prof. H.S. Bhola of Indiana University. One of the most rewarding experience was consultation with Dr Punya Mishra, in Michigan State University. As a specialist of educational technology, he organized a consultative group in the university. What was received from him is the output of the process of consultation with several academicians and educationists.

We had several small group meetings and consultations with many scholars and administrators. A statement by Dr Sugata Mitra, an eminent specialist in ICT and Senior Vice-President of NIIT stands out, and proves prophetic today. In a small group meeting also involving the Joint Secretary, an otherwise articulate Mitra was silent. On insistence he said, 'I have been hearing everyone very carefully. What I gather is we have a solution and we seem to be searching for the problem. And the day we find it we can marry them, and face of India will change'. Indeed, we seem to be still searching for the problem when the solution cries in the sky.

Dr. Malaya Goswami, a consultant with rich international experience in project designing was involved at this stage. We drafted the project together and we submitted the project report in May 2004. Since the project report have remained under consideration of the government, it would not be prudent to provide details of the project, except that the project did not depart from the original concept and approach to its implementation.

We also undertook a few subsidiary activities immediately after submission of the project report. We decided to develop an inventory of software, inspiration came from Sri Gaur. The experience and available documents indicated availability of educational software, particularly in the video and CD format either in higher education produced by EMRC-AVRCs or in elementary education produced by the CIET-SIET network. As mentioned earlier, secondary education happens to be, by far, the most neglected sector. There is no specified agency for developing educational software. We decided to develop a software inventory for secondary education. With the help of Sri Manoj Jain from National Institute of Open Schooling, a comprehensive educational software inventory was developed.

The question was raised about the sources of funding. During such discussions, I proposed a liquid fund for EDUSAT that can be accessed by the states for developing the ground segment facilities, capacity building, etc. on the basis of project proposals from the States. This was not found feasible since states differ on their initiatives as well as capabilities which are true. More importantly, it is the educationally advanced states which are likely to take advantage of this professional approach to financing the project. Government was of the view that it should be supported by a centrally sponsored scheme. Experience of managing different innovative programmes in the country seems to favour centrally sponsored scheme over project based funding. This inability to break away from the convention, even though it does not work is what Prof. William Wry, social anthropologist in Havard University called 'tribalism'—a state of mind. The task came back to me in NIEPA. With the help of Shri M.C. Verma, retired State Education Secretary, we developed a Centrally Sponsored Scheme on EDUSAT covering all universities, colleges and senior secondary schools in the first instance. In the second and third phase, all secondary and elementary schools are to be covered.

In the meanwhile, launching of the satellite was preponed. Instead of March 2005 or even end of 2004, it was launched on September 20, 2004 without any preparation in the ground segment whatsoever.

Elementary Education – Meeting with State ES

In this overall scenario of slow preparation on the ground segment, a refreshing experience was the leadership of Ms Kumud Bansal, Secretary, Department of Elementary Education in the Ministry of Human Resource Development and her colleague Sri K M Acharya, now Additional Secretary. Through a series of meetings, discussions, negotiations, with the national institutions and ISRO, they framed up a fairly comprehensive proposal to cover all District Institutes of Education and Training with two-way interactive facilities. She also convened a meeting of Secretaries and other senior officials from the state governments. Considerable amount of enthusiasm was demonstrated in this meeting.

While elementary education made some progress under the initiative of Ms Bansal, Gaur alerted the deficiency in planning in secondary education where committee did not produce a leaf. I had a one-to-one meeting with him in his office. My contention was secondary education has a natural network, it only needs activation almost without any expenditure. There are about 8,000 private schools affiliated to CBSE and ICSE; then there are about 1250 Kendriya Vidayalayas and Navodaya Vidyalayas. Private schools would not need any government funding; they need to be involved and asked to install the reception facilities. KVs and NVs are not only best of the schools but are also financially well provided by the government. They too should be able to afford Rs. 2.50 lakhs from their annual budget for installing the SIT terminals. At his instance, I submitted a brief note. I personally spoke with the leaders of the private schools; also addressed one of the meetings of National Progressive Schools Conference in one of their member schools on this subject. There was definite evidence of enthusiasm and commitment. There was a meeting with the leaders of the private schools in the Ministry. This was followed up with a meeting in the NCERT headed by the Joint Director of NCERT. This initiative too fizzled out, and nothing actually happened. Yet, when I involved KVS in a programme of NIEPA in a demonstration programme with KV principals in ten centres all over the country through interactive television from IGNOU studio, principals as well as the Joint Commissioner were thrilled with the experience. Commissioner had already indicated his enthusiasm when planning the programme with me in NIEPA.

Pilot Projects

An interesting dimension of the entire EDUSAT episode was the way ISRO planned it out. Though ISRO's role was launching the satellite and MHRD was to look after the educational applications, including setting up the ground segment, it was ISRO that allocated several crorers (I understand about Rs. 90 crores) for pilot experimentations on ground. ISRO set up a pilot project in Chamrajnagar in Karnataka with RoT for elementary education with uplinking facilities located in DSERT Bangalore. Second project was with Venkateswara Technological University with two-way video interactive SIT terminals for technical and engineering education. Another pilot was in teacher education with YCMOU. Other such experimental sites were Anna university in Chennai and Rajiv Gandhi Technological University in Bhopal. ISRO also had dialogues with MP Academy of Administration, IIT Guwahati, and others. It should be noted that ISRO experimented with existing educational institutions that belong to education departments of the government.

Compared to that, education sector did not allocate any fund for EDUSAT; nor did it undertake any pilot project on its own. The only exception was one experiment by the NCTE; commissioned to a commercial outfit it produced a wasteful miserable experience. On the contrary, in every joint meeting with the ISRO, the main effort of the Education sector was to derive funds out of ISRO's fund for pilot experiments.

National Core Committee

The project document provided for creation of a national authority and state authorities for managing educational satellite. This was either not found favour with or was not found feasible immediately. Fact remains that when the satellite was moving in the orbit, there was neither any ground segment facility nor any organizational mechanism that could determine when and how such a facility would be created. I suggested in one of the meetings attended by Dr. Madhavan Nair, the new chairman of ISRO, to appoint a full-time officer, Officer on Special Duty, for EDUSAT in order to move with speed. I also suggested a senior IAS officer to be drafted on a time bound assignment for the job to mobilize the states, move the central government for additional funds. By all means, the service cadre officers were the best bet in the given situation. This did not happen as we would see it later as well. As new institutions were brought into this forum for discussion, several interesting developments happened.

IGNOU provided an important anchoring point for EDUSAT. IGNOU, with its EMPC studio funded by Japan, stood out with its physical facilities compared to that of the NCERT and UGC. There was a change in the government at the Center. Although it affected NCERT rather severely, IGNOU remain unaffected, its leadership executed a smooth turn around and came to the center stage. Importantly, leadership in IGNOU was in a position to give the confidence to the government and take charge of the entire project.

Government constituted a National Core Committee chaired by the Vice-Chancellor of IGNOU; Director DECU, Secretary UGC and I were members.

Compared to the recommendations in the concept document, National Core Committee missed out on the representation of NCERT, NIOS, NCTE, AICTE, ICAR, and ICMR. It was through repeated interventions, that we were able to co-opt other national institutions into the National Core Committee. The major debate in the National Core Committee and elsewhere was around two issues, namely choice of technology – between interactive terminal (SIT) and receive only terminal (RoT), and content generation and pedagogy of interactivity.

Despite the urgency, there were very few meetings of the NCC, I guess not more than three or four during the entire period of six/seven months. It had two-fold effect. The positive effect was preparation for setting up the national channels in school education (NCERT), open and distance education (IGNOU), elementary education including teacher training (IGNOU), technical and management education (AICTE), teacher education (NCTE), agricultural education (ICAR), etc. The negative effect was missing the very spirit of EDUSAT – forest for the trees.

The preparation did not address the issue of generating the state channels as proposed in the original document that could provide education through regional languages. The original concept document provided two channels each for science and technology education for all, language learning, youth channel, executive career channel, gold channel for the senior citizens, channel for women's development, heritage channel, toddlers' channel, and health channel. These channels were primarily conceptualized to provide education to the citizens of India from all walks of life. Each channel could have been the responsibility of certain designated institutions or departments. For example, the Central Institute of English and Foreign Languages with rich experience in providing language learning through radio and television can be responsible for language learning; the section in the Department of Science and Technology that deals with popularization of science can take charge of the channel for science and technology for all; the Department of Women's Development, Department of Health can be responsible for the channels for women's development and health, respectively. This can be achieved only by involving all such agencies into an inter-ministerial framework which was conceptualized in the Satellite Based Educational and Instructional Technology Authority (SIETA).

IGNOU took an initiative in content generation. It asked its faculty members to record lessons. Most of these were extempore, and not necessarily restricted only to the best of the communicators only. Such software will find it difficult to stand the scrutiny of quality under the same set of criteria that IGNOU was evaluating educational software collected from national and international sources for the Gyandarshan Channel.

Only recently, Education Secretary (Secondary and Higher Education) in the Ministry of Human Resource Development chaired a meeting on EDUSAT. EDUSAT may recieve a new thrust. For success, however, EDUSAT would had a need management paradigm.

Conclusion

There are two different faces of development so far. One is the development at the instance of ISRO. It is characterized by achievements before time, holistic thinking as indicated by launching pilot projects and proactive management approach by offering technical and financial support. The development in education is characterized by slow pace, loss of vision and restricting the growth through centralized management.

NOTES

1. I was then Joint Director, NIEPA and not head of an institution; and Ministry of Human Resource Development was not familiar with my involvement in documentation of the concept.
2. Prof. Jaya Indiresan was involved in organizing and developing the report of the National Consultation.
3. As learnt later, this contention was not correct. Large volume of software for secondary school grades are available from private software vendors.
4. DECU developed a comprehensive list of private software producers and vendors, later.
5. This was later recalculated to find the cost of SIT to be approximately Rs 2.40 crores.
6. At this point, I humbly submitted that I have worked in this area for the last more than two decades; subject to his permission, I wanted to present my latest book, Educational Technology: Knowledge Assessment. He not only received with great grace but obliged me with his comments. His comments in another copy are a treasure today.

4

Major Issues

Introduction

Between January 2002 and June 2005, there have been some interesting developments in EDUSAT, though the net result is not very encouraging. It has generated a very fertile ground to learn. In this chapter, I propose to deal with a few major issues.

Pedagogy

All three elements of technology converge on the issue of pedagogy of learning. The RoT, in a way, refers to broadcast alone. Extensive reviews of research indicate that educational television programmes in India are grossly underutilized. Wherever these are used, there is no perceptible, leave alone significant, impact on learning although large number of children express their liking for the educational television programmes[1]. This is borne out by the study by Dr Parhar. Government of India, Ministry of Human Resource Development, commissioned me to evaluate the Educational Technology Scheme – a Centrally Sponsored Scheme launched after the National Policy on Education 1986. The nationwide survey revealed that not more than eight per cent of working television sets is actually used.

On the basis of such research and experience that has accrued since early 1960s, in my assessment, RoT will face the same fate as broadcast television has experienced. It will be a waste of hard earned national resources. I drew the attention of the decision makers to these experiences and research evidences during various interactions. I also drew attention of the members of the committee to the other experience – significant learning gains in case of interactive programmes or animated programmes that create opportunities for interaction among students or between students and teachers after the broadcast.

The second issue was content generation. There was an overwhelming concern for generation of contents in the form of CD-ROM which is needed either for one-way presentation or for computer-based interactive learning. This is needed for a presentational one-way communication. In the project report, we recommended different interactive pedagogy that is not only feasible and practical but also educationally more sound. The knowledge assessment on the contemporary developments of educational technology[2] indicate two major trends in instructional science and technology. These are multi-channel learning and constructivist approaches to learning.

The constructivism is built into the multi-channel learning system. Multi-channel learning system comprises multiple learning channels or opportunities to suit the learning styles of students at various levels and at various ages. Such channels can be used either as stand-alone or in combination with one another depending upon the educational goals and learning styles of the learner. EDUSAT provides at least the following channels:

- Virtual classrooms through two-way videoconferencing,
- Educational broadcast with or without interactive facilities,
- Virtual classrooms through computer conferencing – both real time as well as asynchronous,
- Digital storage and retrieval of educational software at convenience, and
- Internet supported interactive learning.

Virtual Classroom Mode

The discussions on the pedagogy of EDUSAT indicated little concern about the scientific developments in human learning. The tendency is to put more trust on the personal experiences of those who succeeded through the education system without realizing how this unscientific pedagogy pushes out more than 90 per cent children admitted in standard one from the school success zone – less than 8 per cent of all children admitted in grade I actually pass out of higher secondary education, and a large majority of students entering the university level perform very poorly in their learning tasks. The tenor of discussions in such meetings reminds one of George Brown's book 'The Mobile Professor' – where a specialist in Chemistry finds it difficult to respect discipline of physics, or even a high order specialist in one branch of physics finds it difficult to appreciate the contribution of another branch of physics to human knowledge. It is important to recognize that instructional science and technology is well researched and well developed science and do not belong to the domain of common sense, as it never was. For making effective use of EDUSAT, scientific principles and practices of interactive learning have to be adopted.

Then, there is the problem of understanding and responsiveness to the science and techniques of interactive instruction. There is non-responsiveness to the science of interactive learning among the uninformed planners and managers of the education system in general, educational technology in particular. There is a common belief and insistence that a teacher in the studio should present for half the time followed by interaction. There is no pedagogical sanction for such an approach. For, it means asking human minds not to be instantly inquisitive and curious; it must allow subsequent contents to overcrowd and make learning victim of retroactive inhibition. To quote an instance, we decided to host a two-way videoconferencing between experts at one end and a group of eminent pedagogical scientists, namely the education professors from different Indian universities at the other end. Both were connected through two-way video interactive facilities. The experts at the teaching end started making the presentation right on time. When a few of the participating professors wanted to ask questions within the first five minutes and seek certain clarification from the experts on the other end, they realized to their dismay that they cannot speak with the experts on the teaching end – the teaching end had switched off their reception facility. Finally, one had to call on the telephone line from outside the studio to the teaching end requesting them to open up their reception facility.

There is no pedagogical or andragogical sanction to this practice of half an hour lecture followed by half an hour question-answer. This is based primarily on the belief that students learn only when taught by the teacher which itself does not have any necessary evidence. Student learning is guided and impacted by a large number of variables; teaching is one of those variables. More significantly, learning is best achieved when a learner's inquisitiveness is met 'on time' which is called "just-in-time solution" in the world of computers. Postponing the question and the interaction for half an hour not only dissuades the learner and he or she loses the question itself but it also creates negative impact on learning due to retroactive inhibition.

An interesting experience was when IGNOU asked me to conduct a class from its studio end for college lecturers. It was part of an extended contact programme; the participants already had the self-instructional material. I was informed by the organizers that I should speak for half an hour, and I should allow half an hour for question-answer. Instead of following the instruction, I opened the session saying that the participating teachers would have already read their lessons. I would fill in five minutes and by that time I should receive questions, comments by fax, phone or e-mail. Within three minutes, I got the communication, and there was a flood of interaction to the extent that at the fiftieth minute, I took out the diskette from my pocket displayed it before the video camera asking for a few minutes of silence to use my PowerPoint presentation which turned out to be a good summary of their interaction except a few new points which did not come up during the discussion with the participants. This, indeed, is the spirit of interactive learning supported by constructivism. The major problem is the lack of understanding of psychology of human learning; and near contempt of instructional science by the people educated in disciplines other than either education or psychology.

The alternative pedagogy is: a few teachers with outstanding teaching skills and competence in a particular subject can be selected. The teachers will conduct the classes in the studio, may or may not be in presence of a live audience, with an uplink facility. The live teaching session will be uplinked. The lessons will be downloaded in the schools or colleges, as the case may be wherever SIT facilities are established. The learner will be able to view the presentation by the teachers on the television screen; and ask questions, make comments, or enter into interaction with the teacher. The learner intervention will be uplinked which the teaching end can view. Teacher will have the facility or option to accept an intervention. However, whenever he/ she decides to accept an intervention, such interaction will be audible and visible to all other learning centres. This will open up all the reception or learning centres and the teaching centres into a virtual classroom across the state and the nation.

The most significant advantage of this pedagogical process is the availability of best of the teachers to all the students in a state or the country. Further, students across the state will be able to interact with one another; this indirectly gives an opportunity for the average and the poor students to be able to interact with the brilliant ones. From the angle of administration and management, to teach a subject at its best through virtual classroom may require five to ten excellent teachers who are available in any state. Hence, this provides a quantum jump into instructional quality, with a paradigm shift in the pedagogical processes.

It is possible that many of the otherwise brilliant teachers may not be familiar with the modern instructional aids. The teacher support material in the form of PowerPoint presentations, computer graphics, animations, etc. can be prepared in advance; the selected teachers can be trained in the use of such kind of aids to enhance their teaching ability. The entire interactive instructional session should be recorded, digitized and stored in a software archive in a server. A learner should be able to access any such session at his or her own time and place. This will automatically become a mechanism of content generation.

In two-way videoconferencing, a reception centre classroom can have either a large screen television, 29 inch, that can comfortably help about 40 to 45 students to view. Alternatively, the reception centre may have a computer terminal with an LCD projector. This can also accommodate about 40 to 45 learners in one single unit. The virtual classroom can have many such units at any given time, creating a large virtual classroom. Although there is no restriction to the size of virtual classroom, empirical evidences indicate that for quality learning, virtual classrooms should preferably comprise not more than 400 learners. Hence, for school level, most relevant would be district level classrooms, for higher education optimal would be state level and for professional education, virtual classroom can be national.

Compared to the two-way videoconferencing, computer-based virtual classrooms require computer terminals, preferably one terminal for a maximum of three or four students. This particular mode of virtual classroom will require significant expansion of availability of computer terminals in schools and colleges. It will, hence, be more expensive. Further, the cultural ethos of teaching-learning process in India demands a teacher figure. Whereas face-to-face classrooms are ideal from the angle of classroom ethos, virtual classrooms through two-way videoconferencing offers the second best choice; but it overcomes this marginal limitations because of significantly different quality of teaching.

Accordingly, right pedagogical choice is two-way videoconferencing based virtual classrooms as the main instructional platform for the school and undergraduate education. Computer-based virtual classrooms are recommended for comparatively higher levels of education, particularly professional education.

Broadcast Mode

Educational broadcast began in India in 1961-62 to supplement the paucity of science teachers, particularly in Delhi. There have been several experiments and reviews on educational broadcast to assess its utilization and effectiveness. As mentioned earlier, the result is not very encouraging. There are several factors associated with such frustrating results. Major ones are:

- Educational television is alien to educational culture,
- Time mismatch between ETV and schools
- Poor quality of educational software,
- Emphasis on enrichment programs rather than curriculum based programs,
- Teachers are unfamiliar (and untrained) with the methods of integrating educational broadcast

programmes with curricular learning in the schools and colleges.

There has been a steady shift in attitude towards television in general and educational television in particular. The channels like National Geographic, Discovery, etc. have provided a different orientation to what educational television can be. Further, there has been some important innovations in building interactivity in the television programmes as evident in the various news channels where the journalists from the field supplement broadcasting from the studio. In many of the educational and entertainment programmes, channels have introduced phone-in facility. Also, extensive cable television network almost throughout the country, even in some of the rural areas, has taken large number of channels to homes for a token payment. This new cultural and technological scenario can be fully exploited and utilized to reconstruct educational broadcast for EDUSAT.

Accordingly, broadcast mode should be used outside the school and college hours, preferably in the evenings, coupled with phone-in facilities so that the viewers can ask questions and seek clarifications; it also implies that there should be a subject expert available in the studio during the broadcast of the programme. Cable operators need to be involved so that programmes can be taken to homes. If the programmes are directly onto the content and curriculum and of quality and relevance, the programme shall be watched by millions and will attract advertisers making cable operation viable. The pedagogy or delivery of education through EDUSAT demands careful planning with open mind and receptivity to science of education and human learning.

Content Generation and Software

Right from the beginning of conceptualization of EDUSAT, concern for educational software was rightly expressed in all corners. Since ISRO went ahead of the education sector in launching pilot projects in number of places covering elementary education in Chamrajnagar in Karnataka, teacher education with YCMOU, Nasik and technical and engineering education with Anna University, VTU, RGTU, DECU was the first to spot the software deficiency. Nonetheless, the cause of concern was also because of lack of documented information on educational software that already existed in the country and unfamiliarity with such documents.

- Educational software has been produced by the network of CEC-EMRC-AVRCs for higher education for the Countrywide Classroom programme. There are more than 10,000 educational video programmes produced and archived for Higher Education.
- An inventory of educational software in elementary education was prepared by Dr Madhu Parhar in a consultancy project of the UNESCO. This software inventory included print as well as non-print material, namely, audio, video programmes produced by the CIET-SIET network, available both in print as well as in electronic format. The document also listed the language or medium of the educational software.
- The four Technical Teachers Training Institutes have developed a fairly wide range of educational software pertaining to technician education.
- Educational software on higher engineering education has been developed by the Centre for Educational Technologies in the IITs.

- NAARM developed software for agricultural education.
- The wide gap is primarily in the area of secondary education. Except National Institute of Open Schooling and CIET, there is no other agency in the government sector that produce educational software for secondary education. However, at a later stage, during developing a software inventory, we realized that there are several private providers in educational software.

It was, however, necessary to recognize one important limitation of the stock of software. These have been produced over a long period of time. Some of them were originally produced in low band, some others in high band and subsequently in beta cam format; and still later in digital format. Because of poor archiving, many of them may not be useable. But more important issue is the quality of the available educational software that directly impact on the learning gains of students.

Private agencies have been producing educational software for K-12 levels. While developing the software inventory for secondary education as mentioned earlier, we noticed that there are more than 300 educational softwares for one single subject covering, grades 5th to class 10th, from one single source.

Though not related to EDUSAT, UNESCO, Bangkok undertook a project on evaluation of Digital Educational Software for the school level. I was called upon to evaluate Indian software. Samples of 50 softwares were evaluated by each country of the region. I reviewed software prepared by

NCERT, NIOS as well as from a few private producers. The result was quite encouraging. The private producers invariably used high end format with computer graphics and animation, etc.

However, a major or more serious issue about software for EDUSAT is in the basic conceptualization of pedagogy of satellite delivered education. The conventional concept of content generation looked at the issue primarily in the form of CDs. More significant and relevant alternative of delivering live lessons by best of the teachers in the country, with teacher support material like PowerPoint presentation, video clippings, graphics and animation for illustrating abstract concepts, etc.; recording, digitizing and archiving such lectures in the National Resource Archival did not find enough space in the discussions. This alternative pedagogy is sounder, less expensive and can provide much greater relevance to the treatment of content closer to the classroom ethos of the country.

Pulling together the available software from the private producers and live presentation of lessons, the cost for content generation can be substantially reduced. In the name of EDUSAT, some efforts are being made in some of the national institutions with inhouse studio facilities to record free-flow lectures as software. Except in the hands of professionals of extraordinary calibre, such recordings without a script or even a plan will not qualify the quality criteria; this will be futile and waste of national resources.

Ground Network

Network forms the backbone for delivering education through satellite. It is important for us is to understand the length and breadth of the network proposed to take the advantage of EDUSAT. In the original concept document, *Educating The Nation: Need for A Dedicated Satellite* (2002), it was envisioned that the network should be able to provide educational coverage to every citizen of India. Within the formal sector, it is proposed to cover every university and university type institution, every college including professional colleges and institutions, every senior secondary school, every high school and every elementary and primary schools. In the original concept paper, the elementary and primary schools were to be equipped with RoT, which is non-interactive. The primary logic was not pedagogical, but administrative. The installations required to cover all primary schools will be more than 700,000. Even a marginal increase in the cost to move from RoT to SIT will imply a huge investment for the country. For all the other educational institutions, it was proposed to provide SITs so that teachers and learners may interact with the teachers and experts at the teaching end. Universities, particularly the affiliated universities, were to be provided with higher grade of technology so that they could open a sub-hub, uplink and deliver educational programmes. That would mean that each university can have its own educational delivery network with its affiliated colleges. The main hub has been proposed to be installed in every state, feeding two channels, one for secondary education and one for higher education. Besides, the state channels, there will be at least six national channels. Such national channels and hubs are to be fed by the NCERT, IGNOU, AICTE, UGC, DST, ICAR, etc.

While projectizing EDUSAT, there was some trimming of the original proposal, primarily for practical considerations and need for phasing out. In the project document, the proposal was to set up at the first instance 65,000 reception centres covering all universities and colleges, and all senior secondary schools in the country as reception centres, except the universities that could have facilities for uplinking as well. The reception centres, about 42,000, installed in the senior secondary schools can also serve the learning needs of students in the secondary and elementary grades from the neighbouring schools in the form of School Complexes that was experimented some decades ago.

The experience on ground is significantly different. Firstly, neither CSS nor any liquid fund could be mobilized within the Ministry of Human Resource Development so far. It had to look primarily upon ISRO, which always came up with a helping hand within its own limited sanctioned budget. The network that has been conceptualized on ground would cover all the DIETs (500) and 100 terminals each with IGNOU, NCERT, AICTE and about 70 with UGC. Out of these, 69 reception centres belonging to IGNOU have been activated. Others are on the way. In all probability, by end of August 2005, all these reception centres networked with IGNOU, NCERT, etc. will be activated. One major bottleneck seems to be the capability of the agency supplying the terminals. If everything works out well, there would be about 1000 reception centres to deliver educational programmes by IGNOU, NCERT, UGC, AICTE, etc.

Secondary education, as mentioned earlier, remains the weakest spot in the hardware installation as well. A large majority of the KVs, Navodaya Vidyalayas, Central Tibetan Schools and the private schools have the capability to install the reception units from their own budget. This can generate a 10,000 strong network without any additional costs.

The title of the EDUSAT document *Educating the Nation* is not a fancy title, it has certain implied meaning. Accordingly, the 72 channels of EDUSAT has provision for learning the culture and heritage, youth development, women's development, children channel, channel for career upgradation and education, channel for ageing population. Unfortunately, this larger concept of EDUSAT has been lost in the dim of conventional mind set concentrating exclusively on the known limited boundaries of four walls of schools and colleges. EDUSAT will loose its meaning, if its wings are trimmed due to lack of imagination and the so called pragmatism. This is a serious fear that people with imagination have to nurture.

Human Resource Development: Capacity Building

The technology configuration provides the basic framework for generating interactive virtual classrooms. However, the actual quality of such classrooms, particularly the quality of teaching learning process, depends exclusively upon the competence of the people, namely teachers and trainers dealing with such virtual classrooms in the teaching end and the facilitating teachers and trainers at the learning end. Right from the beginning of the conceptualization, hence, capacity building of personnel has been flagged as a major issue. Conventional instructional skills even at their best will fall short.

Capacity building programmes are needed for three kinds of personnel. First and foremost are the teachers for the virtual classrooms. The pilot experiments and experiences indicate that a particular set of skills are required to be a successful virtual classroom teacher. Often, a brilliant teacher in a conventional classroom may not fit into the demands of a virtual classroom. They need to be specially trained in communication, and the use of a whole range of instructional support aids and materials. For example, in a virtual classroom, a teacher teaches literally to the camera; he/she misses out on direct feedback of students through their body language in a classroom. An effective virtual classroom teacher actually operates in a simulated condition.

The second category of people who play a key role in the instructional processes in virtual classrooms are the facilitators at the learning end. Once I was conducting a programme on total quality management in education for the principals of District Institutes of Education and Training from IGNOU studio. There were twenty learning ends spread all over the country. The quality of questions and interaction from Ahmedabad studio was significantly higher than all other centres. I not only expressed my appreciation on screen but also asked the secret of such high quality. The coordinator at Ahmedabad end came on the telephone and told us that Professor R H Dave, former Director of UNESCO Institute of Education, Hamburg was there in the studio and facilitating the discussion by assisting the participating principals how to frame good questions. He was also trying to interpret my responses in terms of its content; sometimes he was also interpreting my response in Gujarati for the facility of the participants. This was a very important and enriching experience about the role of facilitators at the learning end.

Another category of people who have to be trained are coordinating resource persons. In each subject, say for a cluster of classes/grades, it will be necessary to have at least 15 to 20 teachers to be trained for teaching from the studio end as virtual classroom teachers. Given the large number of subjects that are offered at the school level, the need for training and capacity building of specialist teachers would be fairly demanding. In the higher and professional education, the task becomes more complicated because of high degree of specialization. Whereas training of the virtual classroom teachers requires intensity, the training of facilitators poses a different kind of problem. It really implies that every teacher in the school and college classrooms must be trained as a facilitator so that the learning is optimized when the programmes are delivered through EDUSAT. That really means orienting all teachers at all levels; and they are about 50,00,000. Indeed, massive but achievable through EDUSAT itself.

At each state and district levels, a group of people have to be trained in coordinating and managing the EDUSAT delivered programmes.

As the programmes are delivered through EDUSAT, the necessity for training skilled workers for day-to-day maintenance of the equipment being installed in different educational institutions will also be perceived. Although the technology is quite sturdy and there is very little failure, there is a need for people trained in certain basic skills for orienting and reorienting the reception disks, etc. En route to the implementation of EDUSAT in large-scale, new challenges for capacity building will emerge; system ought to be prepared for such contingency management. IGNOU has developed a short module for such skill training. Such training module should be suitably linked with the related vocational education programmes offered either by IGNOU or NIOS to provide legitimacy to the training and the skill so developed.

Cost and Funding

Costing and budgeting for EDUSAT were done at three different points of time. At the first instance, the costing was done in the conceptual document. The cost and financial implications were recalculated at the stage of projectization. A more realistic projection was made at the third stage when this was converted into a draft centrally sponsored scheme. None of the three exercises, however, considered the cost of the space segment, namely the satellite since it was paid for by the Department of Space.

The change in the costing was largely due to reconsideration of the size of the network. For example, in the conceptual document it was visualized that the network will cover every educational institution from primary to the university level with different reception configurations. On reconsideration, at the project stage, this was restricted to 65,000 terminals, at least to begin with in the first phase. This was, however, maintained in the drafting of centrally sponsored scheme on EDUSAT.

The major components of the cost were:

- Technology
- Maintenance
- Capacity building
- Software generation
- Management + R &D evaluation

The cost of technology will depend upon more than one factor. Firstly, SITs are more expensive than ROT; addition of CORDECT will add to the cost. Cost of hubs is different and large. The second important determinant of cost of technology is the size of the network itself. For example, if the network comprises only of state and district levels as compared to state-district-block-all secondary and senior secondary schools, the cost of technology will be different. In order to cover every university, college, senior secondary and secondary school, the estimated financial requirement will be about Rs 4500 crores. The cost of capacity building for such a large network is estimated to be approximately Rs 100 crores; the estimated cost of software generation will be about Rs 50 crores and that for management and R&D it will be approximately Rs 30 crores. The cost of maintenance can be between 5 to 10 per cent of the cost of technology. In a very crude estimate, the total financial requirement would be about Rs. 5,000 crores to set up the network, maintain it, train and develop personnel, generate software, etc.

A major question is the source of funding. In view of general resource crunch in education, it is not easy to find an additional Rs 5000 crores to support programmes in EDUSAT. The official priority in education is on SSA; besides generally enhancing the finance for SSA, government levied two per cent cess to support the midday meal component. Whereas the requirement has always been pitched at least at six per cent of the GDP, the actual allocation has not crossed 3.8 per cent. In the given situation, it was difficult, if not impossible, to apportion funds for EDUSAT from the existing educational budget. It is, hence, important to consider alternative sources of funding. One, there can be a liquid fund for EDUSAT, which states can access on the basis of proposals. The major advantage of this approach is efficiency in financial management. The major problem or risk in this efficiency based approach is the growing gap between the developed and the underdeveloped states. The developed states are characterized not only by greater technical competence but also greater enthusiasm, responsiveness to technology and innovations. Hence, the developed states are likely to access more funds from the central kitty on EDUSAT. In order to maintain a balance, the alternative is to develop a centrally sponsored scheme on EDUSAT. This has found favour with the government, and it was decided to draft a centrally sponsored scheme for EDUSAT. Although the centrally sponsored scheme on EDUSAT has been drafted, it is being discussed and has a long way to go. Besides the normal procedure of bringing in a centrally sponsored scheme, one major problem is with regard to timing. Normally, a new centrally sponsored scheme is not introduced in the middle of a plan period; India is now in the third year of the 10th five-year plan.

ISRO is also seen as an important source of financing EDUSAT, particularly in the beginning years for setting up the technology network. In fact, ISRO was persuaded to provide 200 reception terminals to the institutions identified by the Ministry of Human Resource Development. ISRO funded the complete technology in number of pilot project sites.

Certain important opportunities also need to be explored. For example, during several training programmes of principals of colleges in NIEPA, I explored the possibility of colleges installing the SIT terminals at a cost of approximately Rs 2.50 lakhs on their own. There was unanimity that colleges can manage the expenditure from their own resources subject to the permission by the state education authorities. During my visits to several states, I broached this idea with the state education secretaries; they corroborated principals' views and said that the state will be happy to allow this expenditure within their own budget. The total number of colleges in the country are more than 15,000; even if 50 per cent of the colleges are able to install the reception sets on their own, it will generate a 7500 strong network. The total number of such terminals including secondary schools mentioned earlier where separate state funding may not be necessary can be between 17,500 to about 25,000.

Management

EDUSAT is not only a massive concept but also its implementation is extremely difficult and complex. Given the variety of levels and institutions in education, people outside the schooling framework and through ages, it needs involvement of a variety of stake holders. Accordingly, original proposal was to set up an EDUSAT Authority. This has, however, not happened till now. Till EDUSAT authority is constituted and given full powers, the administrative choice is to develop a mechanism within the government. One proposal was to engage a senior officer, preferably an IAS, on a full time assignment with EDUSAT, may be initially for a period of two years who can take on board Principal Secretaries and Secretaries of Education in the States. Such administrative network has tremendous potentialities to generate this all-important synergy with the states.

Instead, Government of India set up a National Core Committee with four members – UGC, DECU, I in individual capacity and IGNOU in the chair. It was decided to make DEC in IGNOU to house EDUSAT where one of the professors was to be identified to work full time on EDUSAT. This arrangement is fraught with several risks:

- Firstly, National Core Committee (NCC) must be truly national in character representing different interest groups, particularly states and those who have relevant experiences; the current arrangement is neither national nor core.
- Secondly, various national institutions enjoy different kinds of reputation; there is no tradition of accepting one as leader by the others; it is all the more difficult when leadership role is thrust on to a specialist open learning institute. For example, except the chair, heads of none of the institutes participated in the NCC. Such arrangements are perceived as one up-man ship particularly when leadership is 'designated' and not 'ascribed'.
- Thirdly, DEC in IGNOU did not have its own staff; it has been managed for long with make shift arrangement (only now the post of director has been advertised). The charter of EDUSAT does not match with the charter of DEC. This ad hoc arrangement lacks understanding and seriousness of the magnitude of the challenge in managing EDUSAT.
- Fourthly, management of EDUSAT needs creative mind, those who can 'think out of their hat' as said the Education Secretary in a press interview. This arrangement has landed up EDUSAT to a management mind set deeply entrenched in 'tribalism' as formulated by the Social Anthropologist at Harvard University Prof. William Ury[3].

- Fifthly, and most importantly, thrusting leadership role for such a creative endeavour like EDUSAT to where it does not belong resulted into bottling up the 'good summaritan'. EDUSAT lost its vision of 'educating the nation' (people outside the formal education system), state owned and delivered satellite based education; participative and collaborative management framework; it became another programme of a few national institutions.

Conclusion

Progress of EDUSAT's organizational management at the ground level has naturally been rather slow. This needs to be picked up as early as possible. There seems to be no other alternative but get back to the original concept of inter-ministerial authority and full time staff to look after EDUSAT by different stakeholders, including important national institutions that can play their role freely and equally without subjugating the interests of one another. The only interim arrangement is to constitute a national steering committee headed, may be, by one of the former education secretaries, truly representing different interest groups.

NOTES

1. Please refer to the research references in the chapters on broadcast and educational media in this book.
2. Please refer: *Educational Technology: Knowledge Assessment* by Marmar Mukhopadhyay published by Shipra Publications, 2004.

3. For a more interesting elaboration how mental tribalism stands on the way of implementing creative projects, I recommend my readers to Ricardo Semler's *The Seven-Day Weekend: A better way to work in the 21st Century*, Arrow Books, 2003.

5

Lessons for Management

Introduction

Beginning in the early 2002, EDUSAT travelled more than three and a half years. EDUSAT was launched on the 20 September, 2004 by ISRO, a few months ahead of schedule. It completed uncelebrated first year—one year of its stipulated seven year life. The utilization of EDUSAT, excepting the pilot projects sponsored by ISRO, is, of course, yet to begin. Utilization is linked with the establishment of the reception network, identifying software and capacity building—all in the domain of education. Purely, from the angle of management, Department of Space has succeeded and Department of Education failed in accomplishing the mission of EDUSAT.

Issue is not merely the wastage of hard earned national resources or the foregone opportunity or finding fault and indulging in the 'blame culture' (see Pearn, Mulrooney, and Payne, 1998). Issue is much larger; it pertains to the management of education as the most dominant service sector. In this chapter, we would examine this paradox of success and failure, with the primary objective of deriving lessons for management of such large complex projects.

EDUSAT: ISRO

Let us first count as to what has been achieved so far.

- Dedicated Satellite was launched in September 2004 though it was originally scheduled for launching in March 2005, and earliest in December 2004. ISRO completed its target earlier than scheduled.
- ISRO allocated Rs. 90 crores (approximately) for piloting a few projects at the ground level.
- ISRO planned number of pilot projects to test the feasibility of EDUSAT before launching the EDUSAT with a number of educational institutions like Visvesvarayya Technical University, Rajiv Gandhi Technological University, Yashwant Rao Chavan Maharashtra Open University, DSERT Bangalore. ISRO designed these experimental pilot projects in collaboration with identified institutions covering Primary Education (DSERT, Chamrajnagar), Teacher Education (YCMOU, Nasik), Technical and Professional Education (VTU, RGTU). Although there is no formal evaluative study, the projects are working well (I visited Chamrajnagar and VTU project at DSERT, Bangalore).

I discussed the secrets of success of ISRO with Shri Bhatia, who has been involved with EDUSAT. Department of Space, according to Shri Bhatia, succeeded because of a few strategic components in management of the EDUSAT. These are:

1. Department of Space (ISRO and DECU) operates essentially on project modes. Every project is characterized by a well defined target to be achieved

with certain acceptable level of quality within a stipulated time frame. Beginning with Dr Vikram Sarabhai, Dr. Homi J. Bhabha, Dr. Satish Dhawan, President Prof. A.P.J. Abdul Kalam (then in ISRO) developed this culture of time bound, quality assured achievements. They developed the culture of success.

2. The department also learnt to 'celebrate' failure. When SLV-3 failed, instead of crying on each others shoulder or blaming one another, the Failure Analysis Board of ISRO conducted an intensive research and pinpointed the causes of failure. ISRO never failed again. The department developed a mind set characterized by, what Martin Seligman called, 'learned optimism'.
3. In order to make sure that projects succeed, ISRO deploys a dedicated staff, dedicated finance, and a 'set of dedicated minds', though apparently intangible (see Box 5.1).

Box 5.1. Excerpts from an Interview with President Prof. A.P.J. Abdul Kalam in The Hindu, July 25, 2005 by T.S. Subramanian

The second point is, in 1972, both Prof. Satish Dhawan and Prof Brahm Prakash called me. Dhawan said, "I am going to give you a very important project. You will be the Project Leader or Project Director for the first SLV-3. I will give you the required budget. We must do it in seven years. All man power will be available to you from the organization—from all the centres. We will all work together. **Even the Chairman will work for the programme** (emphasis added by the author). It is a very important programme.

When he selected me, I felt a big responsibility. "How am I going to do it?" I had a lot of hesitation. Then Prof. Dhawan gave me a piece of advice. I still remember it. "Kalam", he said, "if one does not do anything, he does not experience any problem. But if you do any mission, any task, problems will arise. That problem should not become your master. You should become the master of the problem, defeat that problem and succeed."

The most important thing is that we were in a position to locate how the failure occurred. M.R. Kurup was the Chairman of the Failure Analysis Board. The present ISRO Chairman, G. Madhavan Nair, was its Member Secretary. He was working with me as one of the project chiefs for the SLV-3. Kurup interviewed more than 125 scientists and staff (about the failure). He analysed over 200 data records.

Kurup and Nair reviewed many of the recommendations of deviation boards and came out with a report within three months of the event. They could technically pinpoint the failure of the air-conditioning plant, which led to dust entering the valve system of the control power plant, resulting in its improper functioning. With the precision diagnosis of the failure, we understand that it was a quality problem and we ensured that all our systems went through rigorous checks. At the same time, I ensured through constant visits to work centres that the motivation of the scientists was maintained at the highest level at all times. These two actions enabled us to go for the next launch within one year and succeed.

After my presentation of the first draft of the conceptual document in Pune followed by appreciations and suggestions for improvement, Dr. E.V. Chitnis, an eminent space scientist and a former member of the ISRO team, asked, "Whose Head will role if the project fails?" There was a meaningful smile on the face of every one from the Department of Space. Obviously, we (belonging to the education sector) had never heard such a question. I tried to find out the import of the question. Shri Bhatia told me, "like any other department, people in ISRO are also on government job. They will not loose their jobs if they don't perform and the project fails; but imagine the embarrassment of the people who become responsible for the failure, and imagine this within the cultural and organizational ethos of success. There is an element of accountability, which is part of the organizational culture of ISRO." It makes lot of sense. Failing in a culture of failure is normal; people get desensitized and learn to reduce expectations and targets. In a way, they develop the mindset of 'learned helplessness' (Seligman, 1990) and tend to justify failure.

Finally, it is interesting to note that ISRO sponsored number of pilot projects on EDUSAT in the education sector though its primary responsibility comprises design, production and launching of satellite. In order to ensure success, ISRO set up its own learning laboratory in the form of pilot projects. This, too, is part of the culture of success.

EDUSAT: Education

The issue of management of EDUSAT can be examined under a few specific heads like vision, strategic planning, networking and software, financing, and organization and leadership.

Vision

As mentioned in the previous chapter, EDUSAT was visualized as an instrument of 'educating the nation'. The channel count, accordingly, was not a simple arithmetic. It had a built-in vision. As many as 54 channels were allocated for school and higher education; both formal and distance education.

Remaining channels were visualized to be allocated for education in languages, culture, women's development, health, youth development, of on-the-job training for career advancement, old age and children, etc. In tune with the call of the President, Prof. A.P.J. Abdul Kalam, vision was for transforming India into a learning community that can confidently strive towards the ambition of emerging as a developed nation by 2020.

This vision has been lost. With imprisoned vision, it has been converted into a few national channels for enriching conventional education at the school, higher and professional education, and open and distance education. The forest has been missed for the trees.

The first and foremost task is to reinstall the vision of *educating the nation* that can be achieved only by activating all the 72 channels. Non-feasibility is the usual argument of the 'wise pragmatists' dubbing such massive visions as utopia. It is important to recognize that it is only such necessary utopias that drive a nation to achieve new heights. Visions of Independent India in the deadly depth of British regime or non-apartheid South Africa with Nelson Mandela in jail in apartheid regime were utopias. These are amply perceptible in Gandhiji's autobiography, '*Story of My Experiment with Truth*' and Nelson Mandela's life portrait in, '*Long Road to Freedom*'.

In practical terms, restricting EDUSAT to five or six channels amounts to using less than seven per cent of the total potential of EDUSAT; and an wastage of 93% of the investment in EDUSAT. This is besides the 1/7th cost of EDUSAT having been wasted due to non-utilization for the whole of the first year of its seven year life. More importantly, in the process of this restriction, a vision has been lost—vision of empowering the Indian states with media facilities to deliver education through modern technology and pedagogy in regional languages. It has brought us back by fifty years—centralization of educational media..

The first dimensions of the vision is to make sure the use of all the transponders and channels of the satellite for educating people from all walks of life in the country to generate a learning community.

The second dimension of the vision is the qualitative use of the satellite. The vision is to develop a live vibrant interactive countrywide virtual classroom where learners of all ages and from all walks of life would have access to the best of the experts. This qualitative aspects of vision rejects the conventional concept of educational software in the form of video and audio programmes, digital or otherwise, which is primarily meant for broadcast. In order to make full use of EDUSAT and to achieve the goal of educating the nation, it will be necessary to simultaneously reinstate the quantitative as well as the qualitative aspects of the vision as enunciated in the conceptual and projected documents.

This, however, is easier said than done. According to the available research evidence, vision is a creative faculty of mind which is not evenly distributed; it is rather skewed. On the contrary, a large majority of the people, irrespective of their education and position, suffer from tribalism (sticking to old ways of thinking and working—a formulation by Professor William Ury, an eminent social anthropologist in Harvard University; Semler, 2003). However, the installation of the vision will become possible only when leaders (a concept of the 19th and 20th century) get replaced by 'leadership' (21st century paradigm).

Strategic Planning

A project as massive as EDUSAT requires careful strategic planning. So far, management of EDUSAT has missed professional input of mission guided strategic planning.

Education is on the concurrent list. As a matter of practice, states have larger say on the content and curriculum of education at the school as well as at the college and university levels. Any centralized programme cannot have the appeal, relevance, and impact even for the conventional formal education, particularly when educational mass media (radio and television) is yet to find acceptability among the teaching and the learning community as borne out by several studies including evaluation of Educational Technology Scheme (Mukhopadhyay and Sinha; 1993). Programmes must be decentralized, located and anchored in the states so that students may have access to curricular instruction and learning packages that can help them in performing in the board and university examination (refer President Prof. A.P.J. Abdul Kalam's seminal view on this as expressed during our interview with him on EDUSAT, referred on page 153). Further, education at both school and higher education is imparted largely through the regional languages. Programmes offered through either English or Hindi, through national channels, would have little acceptability and impact on the students. Two important parameters of the strategic planning for EDUSAT is the involvement of the States, and offering programmes through regional languages. These two criteria are interconnected and interdependent; programme offering cannot be done through regional languages without direct involvement of the state level agencies.

States have amply demonstrated their vision and capability to design meaningful programmes, implement and make full use of such innovative techniques. Before EDUSAT was launched, Karnataka set up its own satellite based interactive communication technologies and have effectively used for education, and in other areas of development initiative including women's development. The state of Gujarat has setup a modern interactive videoconferencing facility spread through out the state that is being actively and effectively utilized for capacity building. Madhya Pradesh set up its own network connecting all the districts with two-way audio and one-way video conferencing facility from Bhopal.

Institutions like Indian Institutes of Technology in Kharagpur and Powai, in particular, have been offering online education. Sponsored by ISRO, VTU, RGTU, YCMOU, are offering interactive programmes in technology and teacher education, respectively. There are several institutions in the private sector like NIIT, APTECH, etc. that offer interactive online education. An important attribute of a quality strategic planning is to involve the people with experience and expertise in the field. Restricting implementation of EDUSAT to a select few at the national level will cause serious damage to the innovative concept and potential of EDUSAT.

Networking and Software

The vision as well as the project document visualized an interactive (SIT) network connecting all universities, colleges, senior secondary and secondary schools; all elementary and primary schools with Receive only Terminals (RoT). Obviously, this large network can neither be implemented at one go; nor is it necessary. Question is not of money alone; there are several associated dimensions including system capability. The strategy has been to offer terminals, usually about 100 to IGNOU, NCERT, AICTE, UGC, ICAR, etc. at their own cost (please visit website edusat@ignou.ac.in). This, even if successfully implemented, will create some kind of 'monopoly channels' for each of the national institutions; leaving the vision and mission of EDUSAT as a participative mechanism for generating a learning community unfulfilled. This management approach has not worked; there are not enough funds and or system capability to establish even a fragment of the proposed network on time. It needs a different management strategy for developing the ground network.

As a matter of strategic planning of the network, the first level network should be connecting the state capitals (one of the state level institutions identified by the state government) with one of the national nodes—institutions like IGNOU, NCERT, AICTE, UGC, etc. This will be achieved in the strategy adopted now. The second level network should include districts (e.g. DIETs). Under DPEP, a large number of DIETs have been provided with digital one-way video two-way audio interactive reception facilities. Such facilities can be upgraded with necessary modification to receive and transmit video signals. This largely was the decision arrived at in the meeting chaired by Education Secretary in charge of elementary education in the Ministry of Human resource Development, Government of India. The network has not, however, been functional, so far. Subject to verification, we understand that the agency commissioned by DECU for supplying the reception equipments is unable to cope with the challenge.

There are about 10,000 senior secondary schools—private schools, Navodaya Vidyalayas and Kendriya Vidyalayas. Most of such schools have the necessary financial strength and capability to install the reception facilities without the government support. To begin with, the secondary education network can comprise of these schools. The higher education network, comprising the universities and colleges, can also be set up largely at their own cost. During projectization of EDUSAT, I had extensive consultations with the principals of colleges and State Education Secretaries in charge of higher education. More than 70 per cent of the institutions of higher education are financially capable of installing interactive reception facilities without additional government grant. What has been missed out in the management of EDUSAT is mobilization of multiple sources to generate a synergy. It has chosen to depend almost exclusively on central funding through a Centrally Sponsored Scheme which is very difficult to introduce in the middle of a plan period.

There is an endless uninformed debate about the non-availability of software; that is put forward as the primary reason for non-utilization of EDUSAT. This is a completely misplaced argument. It is besides the point that there is a good stock of software in higher education, as well as in secondary and elementary education as is evident from the software inventory developed under the EDUSAT project, and documentation of the software by CEC. The pedagogical vision of EDUSAT is, as mentioned earlier, developing a vibrant live interactive countrywide virtual classroom where learners will have direct access to eminent teachers and experts not only to listen to their presentations but also to interact with them. In such presentations, the experts and teachers may need certain support material like PowerPoint presentation, video clippings, audio clippings, computer animation, etc. Such teacher support material can be developed at much lower cost with greater efficiency and speed. The conventional '22 minute programme' software is required for broadcast which is not the pedagogical agenda in EDUSAT. On the contrary, the vision is to digitize and archive such expert presentations along with interactions for retrieval at convenience and necessity.

Finance

Financing for establishing the ground level network for EDUSAT has been sought to be achieved through conventional methodology of mobilizing additional funds from the government sources. Instead of efficiency driven liquid funds, the decision has been in favour of a centrally sponsored scheme for EDUSAT, as mentioned above. It is important to mention that several centrally sponsored schemes were launched in education particularly after the National Policy of Education and Programme of Action, 1986. Evaluation of the centrally sponsored schemes including Educational Technology, CLASS, etc. has reveled a common pattern—centrally sponsored schemes have not provided the desired results. The choice has been in favour of centrally sponsored scheme much largely because the system is used to implementing projects through centrally sponsored scheme. The important lesson for management, as demonstrated by the Department of Space, is to learn from the failed strategies.

There is very good chance of generating financial resources for developing ground level network by mobilizing multiple sources. For example, for developing the network connecting the national hubs with States and district centers can be managed through SSA. Between 2003-04 and 2004-05, the funding for SSA rose from about Rs. 7,000 to more than 13,000 crores. During the meeting of the Governing Council of SSA, Prime Minister assured adequate funds for implementation of SSA. SSA, by itself, has fairly strong provision for capacity building of teachers. Interactive videoconferencing through EDUSAT can provide a quantum leap to quality of capacity building programmes. This network can be used for other purposes till alternative networks are developed. Similarly, the network for the colleges and universities can be largely developed through self financing; alternatively, may be with marginal support from the Government of India through UGC.

Such alternative approaches to mobilization of funds and management of financial resources for EDUSAT needs to be given a fair trial.

Organization and Leadership

EDUSAT is a complex massive project. It has also to be time bound in order to be socially accountable, and effective. The document suggested, after careful consideration and consultation with large number of people, setting up of a National Authority for managing EDUSAT. Instead, government decided to set up a national core committee comprising of only four members. It was, however, neither 'national' nor 'core'. It could not involve states, set up the minimum ground level infrastructure. When urgent business like approach was required, the committee met only thrice (2nd and 31st December, 2004, and 25th May, 2005, besides a meeting chaired by Education Secretary on 19th July, 2005)—far too infrequently to push the project forward. From the angle of processes, such meetings were archaic with little scope for generating creative solutions for problem solving.

Let us imagine an alternative management framework, at least till such time the EDUSAT Authority is established and becomes functional.

Government can constitute a National Steering Committee that is of truly national character comprising representatives of major national institutes and all those institutions engaged in EDUSAT Pilot Projects sponsored by ISRO, Education Secretaries of one state each from the five regions with a full-time Secretary chaired by a former Union Education Secretary (ISRO appointed one of the retired IAS officer as a fulltime consultant/advisor to EDUSAT). One of the national institutions can act as the secretariat to the committee the way NIEPA and NCERT hosts many such committees. The committee can be given a dedicated fund, howsoever small or big, the way Ministry of Human Resource Development provided funds for the CABE Committees, Minority Education Commission, etc.

Without such broad-based committee, it will not be possible to mobilize and involve the States. Without active involvement of the states, EDUSAT will find it difficult, if not impossible, to achieve its mission. It is necessary to understand and recognize that states are the critical success factor for EDUSAT.

The second important dimensions of organization and management of EDUSAT is the staff. Effort has been made to manage such a massive project without full-time dedicated staff; instead part-time staff has been drafted from within the university where the project has been parked. Implementation of EDUSAT has to be full-time business of a team of competent and dedicated professionals as has been the case with DECU.

It was decided to park EDUSAT at DEC in IGNOU. Tagging a massive project like EDUSAT with one university and housing it in one of its component units without adequate staff resembles efforts to store million gallon health drink in a 5ml tea cup. This management strategy has cost EDUSAT dearly during the last one year. It has saved couple of lakhs of rupees on staff cost draining out nearly 150 crores by non-utilization of EDUSAT. A bad economics, indeed. Howsoever competent the university may be, it has its own business to attend. EDUSAT cannot be at the centre stage in the university. No wonder, EDUSAT received only residual attention of those who could be spared without affecting the functioning of the host institution. This experience is not new. As long as NCTE functioned from NCERT (secretariat), it was hardly known; NCERT had a far larger agenda—entire school education—where NCTE was for quality management of teacher education that was one of the many departments of NCERT. Similar are the cases with AICTE and NAAC. EDUSAT is still different; it is larger than IGNOU since its vision was to cover every citizen of the country. It was larger than all educational institutions put together.

Strategically, the arrangement does not get accommodated within the ethos of the national institutions. History and tradition indicate that the national institutions do not accept hierarchical relationships amongst themselves. They are equals. This is evident from the fact that hardly ever any head of a national institution attended the meetings of the National Core Committee. In fact, such an arrangement alienates other national institutions leaving this as the business of the host institution chosen by the government. On the contrary, scenario changes whenever the meetings are called by the Education Secretaries.

Management of EDUSAT, as mentioned repeatedly, has to involve the States and state-level institutions. Except for a competent full-time team, independent of any particular institution, management of EDUSAT will continue to limp. It will be necessary to set up a full-time organizational set up dedicated to implementation of EDUSAT. Such an organization can be physically located in a hired accommodation as is the case with many national institutions, e.g. NIOS, NCTE, AICTE, etc. or, in one of the national institution without any reporting relationship to the concerned organization.

There have been some efforts for coordination and management of EDUSAT. At the national level, an Inter-departmental Programme review Board (PRB) has been constituted by Chairman ISRO. PRB comprises, other than ISRO Officials and scientists, Secretary of MHRD, Chairman UGC, Vice-chancellor of IGNOU, VTU, Amrita Viswa Vidyalaya, Director of NCERT. The notable missing name is NIEPA, the apex planning and management institution in education that drafted the concept document, project document, CSS Scheme document and software inventory, and hosted the national consultation. Besides the PRB, as mentioned earlier, there is a National Core Committee, now extended to accommodate more members.

Chairman ISRO has also appointed a EDUSAT Utilization Project Management Board (PMB) and a Direction and Guidance Project Management Council (PMC) comprising scientists and administrators from the Department of Space.

There is a proposal to set up a State Core Group (decided in the meeting of the State education secretaries in September and October, 2004). However, such core committees are, after more than a year, yet to see the light of the day though 21 states have identified a nodal officer for EDUSAT.

Finally, organization and management is the function of leadership. Leadership has caused the crisis right from the beginning; it has been the most decisive reason for the management failure so far. To begin with, when EDUSAT was presented by Dr. Kasturirangan to the then Minister of Human Resource Development in presence of the senior officials from the Ministry of Human Resource Development and heads of national institutions, exceptions apart the body language of the planners and administrators of education was characterized by reluctance. The excitement of Dr. Kasturirangan and officials of ISRO was not reflected in their counterparts from education. Commitment seemed to be 'this too shall be on done, if we have to'. Literally, nothing happened, not even any discussion for more than one year from the presentation by Dr. Kasturirangan. As mentioned earlier, it is out of desperation, and at the instance of Shri Bhatia, DECU and NIEPA organized the national consultation on EDUSAT. Yet, nothing happened. Only after a gap of more than one year of the National Consultation, Joint Secretary (Secondary Education) was asked to look after EDUSAT in addition to all his other duties. It is much later that IGNOU entered the scene.

Management literature indicates that a large majority of the people in leadership positions in universities and such institutions are either administrators or managers. Very few have visions and dreams that qualify themselves to be leaders.

Leaders are the institution builders. Managers manage the status quo. No wonder that institution builders are rare (Latchem and Hanna, 2001 and Mukhopadhyay, 2004).

The loss of vision and absence of strategic planning are the indicators of leadership crisis. It is the low-vision that tailored EDUSAT from an instrumentality of creating a one-billion strong learning community to one more tool in distance education. An extraordinary idea has been trivialized to ordinariness. In Daniel Goleman's paradigm, EDUSAT leadership is commanding and feudal, one of the dissonant styles. Leadership style was exclusive, when it warranted inclusive leadership. Contrast this with the resonant and inspiring style in the Department of Space—'*All manpower will be available to you from the organization—from all the centres. We will all work together. Even the Chairman will work for the programme*", said Dr. Satish Dhawan and Dr. Brahm Prakash when they called upon Shri A.P.J. Abdul Kalam to take charge of SLV-3 as stated by President Prof. A.P.J. Abdul Kalam in his interview with The Hindu (Box 5.1).

What kind of leadership is required for implementing a massive imaginative project like EDUSAT? The newly emerging research evidence demands resonant (Goleman 2002), inspirational (Secretan 1999), and L-5 (self-evasive) leadership (Collins, 2001). Management of EDUSAT must find leadership dedicated to the vision suited to culture of efficiency, and committed to inspirational style.

Conclusion

EDUSAT is unconventional. It cannot be managed by conventional management approaches. It cannot be managed by people who are entrenched within their own institutional framework, and cocooned within administrative 'tribalism'. It cannot be managed with myopic vision. It will need, as the Union Education Secretary rightly said, 'people who can think outside their hats'. It will be necessary to follow the footsteps of ISRO to construct utilization of EDUSAT in a project mode with dedicated authority, dedicated staff, dedicated fund and a culture of social and economic accountability.

There is a rich stock of experience in managing such projects in different parts of the world as indicated in a chapter on international experience in interactive television (Parhar, 2006). There are some outstanding experiences in managing massive projects in mission mode in India. What is needed is an open minded approach to learn from previous experiences.

REFERENCES

Collins, J., *Good to Great*, New York: Harper, 2001.

Goleman, D. *et al.*, *The New Leaders: Transforming art of Leadership into Science of Results*, Little Brown, London, 2002.

Latchem, C. and Hanna, D., *Leadership for 21st Century Learning: Global Perspectives from Educational Innovators*, Kogan Page, London, 2001.

Mukhopadhyay, Marmar & Sinha, N. Utilization of Media in Education (a commissioned Study by Ministry of Human Resource Development), New Delhi: NIEPA, 1993.

Mukhopadhyay, Marmar and Indiresan, Jaya, *National Consultation on EDUSAT*, New Delhi: NIEPA, 2003.

Mukhopadhyay, Marmar, *Leadership for Institution Building in Education*, Baroda: SERD, 2004.

Parhar, Madhu, *Satellite in Education: Critical Knowledge Base for EDUSAT*, New Delhi: Shipra, 2006.

Pearn, M., Mulrooney, C. and Payne, T., *Ending the Blame Culture*, Hampshire: Gower, 1998.

Secretan, Lance (1999), *Inspirational Leadership: Destiny, calling and cause*, Toronto: Macmillan Canada.

Seligman, Peter, M. (1990), *Learned Optimism: How to Change your Mind and your Life*, New York: Pocket Books, 1990.

Semler, Ricardo, The Seven Day Week End: Finding the work/life balance, London: Century, 2003.

APPENDIX – I

Space for Education: Progress in Partnership

*Inaugural Address**

I had the honour of presenting the EDUSAT plans to the Hon Minister for Human Resource Development Professor Murli Manohar Joshj, and we were greatly heartened by the enthusiastic support from him. We have had several discussions with different agencies of Ministry of HRD, eminent academicians, faculty of NIEPA and many others and have been encouraged by their support. I am glad to be here for the National Consultation where a large number of eminent educationists and scientists have come together to discuss the utilization of EDUSAT.

ISRO has always aimed at using space technology for socio-economic development of the country. That no nation can make progress in the real sense, without a sound EDUSAT system hardly needs reiteration. How to achieve progress in the field of education, how technologies can help in accelerating this development, what should be the special role of Space Technology are some of the issues that need to be discussed jointly by the educationists and scientists.

One of the biggest contributions of satellite technology is in expansion of the reach even to the remotest regions of the country. The quick and simultaneous reach brings about not only a quantum jump but a basic qualitative change. The New Information and Communication Technologies (NICTs) have revolutionized the reach and quality of information dissemination and the space programme of the country can take legitimate pride for achieving this. The revolutionary change in the television and telecommunication scenario, which we have witnessed in the last decade or so, is a striking example of this revolution.

Space for Education: Progress in Partnership

ISRO has undertaken several projects and programmes to promote the cause of education. The partnership of ISRO and MHRD goes way back to early 70s when the preparations for Satellite Instructional Television Experiment (SITE) were underway. This biggest techno-social experiment in the world marked the beginning of the satellite-broadcasting era in the country. More importantly, it marked the beginning of a long and sustained collaboration between our departments.

SITE

SITE conducted in 1975-76 overcame the barriers of distance and remoteness by reaching 2500 villages spread in 6 states of the country. Ministry of Education was a leading user in SITE and it contributed to the programme in several very significant ways. There were programmes for School Children and School Teachers. Nearly 50,000 teachers were trained in Science Education during SITE. Science programmes for rural children formed an important component of SITE transmission. NCERT was involved in the conduct of several research studies on the impact of SITE on Education.

Jhabua Development Communications Project-Interactive/ TDCC

The Jhabua Development Communications Project (JDCP) combined Broadcasting and Interactive Training Programmes. The evening broadcasts had a large number of programmes explaining the importance of Education and encouraging children to attend school and motivating parents to send children to school. The Interactive Training Programmes trained a large number of teachers, updating teaching skills and updating them on the contents.

Training and Development Communication Channel

Training and Development Communication Channel (TDCC) in operation since 1995 is an Interactive one-way video, two-way audio communication channel. It is very widely used countrywide by the Education Departments, Universities, Engineering Colleges and Agriculture Universities. It is extensively used for primary school teachers training by DPEP.

Educational Programmes on Other Networks

The Indian National Satellite System (INSAT) has been the major catalyst in the rapid expansion of terrestrial television coverage in Indira. INSAT is being used to provide educational TV (ETV) service for primary school children in 6 states. A general enrichment programme on higher education (college sector) is telecast on the National Network. These programmes provided by the University Grants Commission (UGC), are a part of its countrywide-classroom programme. The Indira Gandhi National Open University (IGNOU) broadcasts for half-an-hour daily via the National Network, curriculum based lectures for the students of the Open University.

Gyan Darshan is an exclusive educational TV channel of India started in January 2000 by IGNOU, MHRD and Prasar Bharati. At present Gyan Darshan has four channels: GD Channel, Interactive Distance Education, Eklavya Technology Channel, and Gram Bharati.

Apart from these, Gyan Vani is educational FM Radio of India.

Education: The Backbone of National Development
Credo of Education

Education embraces all aspects of life. It has influence over the individual, the society and the nation as a whole in several different significant ways. Education is holistic and covers all dimensions of life; education is a life long process. The challenge is to remain updated and create a knowledge based nation and society.

Achievements

Education is described as the backbone of national development. India has made tremendous progress in this field since independence. The literacy rate has crossed 60 per cent and India has the third largest scientific manpower in the world. It is a leading nation in the field of Information Technology. There are nearly 250 universities, 12,000 colleges, practically every village has a school, the enrolment is cent per cent, and women have entered practically every occupation. There are significant achievements in the fields of science, literature, arts and other creative fields. There are many other areas of progress that can be enumerated.

... but miles to go

In spite of these achievements, there remains much to be done. India has a very large population of illiterates. Female illiteracy and rural illiteracy is 45 per cent. There is a high dropout rate and there is a challenge of the reaching the unreached and bridging the digital divide between the rural and urban populations. The rapid changes due to global explosion in the knowledge field, the need for making education holistic and covering all dimensions of life, increased need for continued education has thrown up several challenges for education. These challenges become very complex because of the pluralistic culture, of multiple languages, customs, religions and other aspects of culture.

Response to the Challenge

There is an urgent need for modernization and adoption of new technologies in education to meet the trim challenge of quantity and quality. Several attempts have been made to use educational communication by different agencies and Ministry of HRD. Bringing about integration of these efforts and building a synergy is a challenge that must be accepted.

EDUSAT

The needs of education are many and varied. It is often observed that educational broadcasting suffers when there is a demand of other sectors like entertainment. It is therefore necessary to have a dedicated educational satellite for this purpose. It is only through such a satellite that one can meet the requirements of education sector without interruption and to suit the specific demands of education. There is need for reaching formal, non-formal and continuing education to the vast masses of this country.

EDUSAT has the technological capabilities of television and radio broadcasting, video conferencing, audio and video return links, computer based data transfer etc. It will supplement curriculum based teaching, provide effective teacher training, facilitate community participation, and enable interaction between scholars and researchers. EDUSAT can enable a major paradigm shift through making education interactive than a mere one way transfer of information. It will be a quantum jump in providing access to education to remote areas and improving the quality of education. It will strengthen the teacher and the administration. It cannot be and has not ever been conceived as a replacement for the existing system of the teacher and the school.

The Space Segment

In order to meet the multifarious challenges of the pluralistic society like ours, ISRO has planned a satellite-EDUSAT-entirely dedicated to the cause of education. EDUSAT will be launched by the third flight of indigenous Geo-Synchronous Launch Vehicle (GSLV)-GSAT-3 by the end of 2004. EDUSAT will have the capability to provide 5 Ku-Band regional beams, 6 channel C-Band and one Ku-Band national beam. Each beam will be capable of providing bandwidth equivalent to 10 digital TV channels. This would facilitate both the national and regional needs to suit particular states and enable imparting of education in the regional languages.

The Ground Segment

The space segment available through a dedicated satellite must be supported with corresponding infrastructural support at the ground level that is at the schools, colleges, universities etc. The ground segment will require-a server and studio at state level Receive Only Terminals (ROTs) or Interactive Terminals to suit the specific requirements of the sector. These can be located in schools, colleges, teacher training institutes, DIETs, blocks or wherever required by the education department. As it is, many of the educational institutes already have a good ICT infrastructure, television sets, PCs etc. The scenario is bound to improve in the days to come and these existing facilities can be utilised to support EDUSAT.

Challenges of Education and Space Technology

It is sometimes argued that satellite technology is a luxury for a country like ours where schools often do not have rudimentary facilities like blackboards, or a proper building to sit in. This argument is not only misleading, it is actually dangerous. The above facilities are needed and must be fulfilled. Satellite per se is not going to meet these requirements. The questions really to be asked are: Can we afford not to use the modern ICTs and the strengths of satellite broadcasting? Can we think of meeting several challenges of education without modernisation? Can we afford to lag behind others in the use of modern communication technologies?

Just think of some of the challenges of education and let us ponder if we can afford not to harness the benefits of space technology? The challenge of education is two-fold-the challenge of numbers and the challenge of quality. It is estimated that out of 200 million children in the age group of 6-14, only 120 million children are enrolled. Out of these nearly 40 million do not attend school. This means that 80 million children have to be brought under the educational umbrella. There is an alarmingly high dropout rate, as many as 87 per cent of children dropout by Grade 12. Dropout of the girl child is a major challenge faced by the nation. Ministry of HRD has launched an ambitious programme called 'Sarva Shiksha Abhiyan' to achieve minimum, universal education by the year 2015, This will mean addition of 45 million students in a short span of time. Won't the space technology help reaching this unreached target? Would it be possible to achieve it without it?

The challenge of quality is another major issue. More than 80 per cent of failures in Higher Secondary Board Exams are in the subjects of Mathematics, Science and English. Nearly 50 per cent of teachers at school levels are educated only up to secondary level themselves. There is a need for continuous training of teachers and to supplement curriculum teaching by experts. There is a shortage of qualified teachers at the higher level education also especially in the field of IT and other frontier areas of knowledge. EDUSAT will go a long way in meeting some of these challenges. I understand that the committee appointed by MHRD for Elementary Education has already submitted a detailed report on utilisation of EDUSAT for teacher education. We need to have specific recommendations like this from other sectors as well.

Content Development and Educational Software

This will be a major challenge for EDUSAT. The success of the project will substantially hinge on this aspect. An educational programme ought to have accuracy of content, its authenticity and credibility. It must be consistent with the syllabus prescribed by the respective education department, university etc. A full time channel would require nearly 25,000 programmes per year. To produce high quality educational software, it will be necessary to upgrade and upscale the in-house programme production capabilities, and develop a network of specialist production agencies for outsourcing. Necessary infrastructure and facilities for this exist in the country. There is no dearth of subject expertise. We have to create a mechanism wherein the expertise and skills of the experts and the media makers get coordinated. This will require innovative management structure and a facilitative organisation.

Management Challenge

The success of EDUSAT will depend upon the extent of the synergy between different stakeholders: Educationists, Instructional Designers, Media Makers, Educational Policy Makers, Administrators, Social Scientists, Teachers

Community, etc. There has to be effective linkage between these different elements.

Several Ministries and Departments will have to come together. Ministry of Human Resources Developments will be a key player and in addition the Department of Space and the Ministry of Information Technology will have to play a key role.

I am confident that these two days of deliberations will go a long way in suggesting ways and means of utilizing EDUSAT in a confident and coordinative manner. Different disciplines will work together and prepare an Action Plan so that EDUSAT becomes an effective vehicle for the spread of education, sow seeds of enlightenment and prepare groundwork for need-based human society.

APPENDIX – II

EDUSAT: All You Wanted to Know

What is EDUSAT?

EDUSAT is the acronym for Educational Satellite—a satellite dedicated to education with as many as 74 channels—brain child of Dr. K. Kasturirangan and carefully nurtured by Development and Educational Communication Unit (DECU) of ISRO under the leadership of Sri B.S. Bhatia; concept and project documentation are contributions of Prof. Marmar Mukhopadhyay of NIEPA. Actually, EDUSAT is a technology network of uplink stations in selected national and state locations (to act as teaching ends), and downlink stations or facilities in various educational institutions (as learning ends) supported by satellite.

How Does it Really Work?

When the teacher teaches in front of the camera in the uplink station, the audio and video signals gets beamed to the satellites. The satellite sends signals back to the earth that can be received by the reception terminals, where the reception dish antennas have been installed and are oriented towards the satellite transponders. The teaching in the studio can now be seen and heard in the classrooms. The classroom is provided either with a large 29 inch television, with a camera and audio equipments, or a computer with an LCD projector and audio equipment. When a learner asks questions the audio and visual signals gets beamed to the satellite which in turn sends it back to the teaching ends. By using the facilities on the console, the teacher can see and hear the student. Also, student will be visible to all the other learners in various others learning ends, creating a virtual classroom.

The network has the facility of recording the lessons taught at the teaching end as well as the questions asked by the learners and store in digitized form in the server. Lessons thus stored can be retrieved by anyone with access to computer. As a result, it will be possible for a student to revisit and relive the classroom experience.

Why do we need it? What is the advantage?

Since independence, India has made tremendous strides in the expansion of educational facilities. The literacy rate of five per cent in 1901 that grew to about 19 per cent in 1951 (in the first 50 years of British regime) grew to more than 65% during the next 50 years. Compared to a few million students in 1951, Indian education now reaches out to more than 196 million students. This enormous gain in enrolment, largely gets reduced by massive drop out at various levels especially between grades I and VIII. Also, students performances are far from satisfactory. Combining the two elements of drop out and performance, what we achieve is: out of 100 children admitted in class I, only about 26 appears for grade 10 examination; 13 pass out; and only about six complete XII grade examination; a large majority of them pass in the third division.

We need a quantum jump in improvement of quality of education. President A.P.J. Abdul Kalam, in his address to the Parliament emphasized the need to build quality in education fast. Technology provides that empowerment to wards building quality in education.

Examine this from our day-to-day experiences. Quality of student learning and performance depend largely upon the quality of teaching in the classroom. There is wide variation in the quality of teachers and teaching from one school or college or university to another. Students have restricted access to a good teacher. In a university or college or a school, some have access to an excellent teacher of mathematics, but not in Geography or English language; and yet some in other institution, reverse may be the case.

Technology network overcomes that important limitation. For teaching say, Mathematics, or Physics or History from the teaching end (uplink station), we need only about 10 excellent teachers who may be strewn around in the schools, colleges and universities. Such excellent teachers can be brought together to teach from the uplink stations, and every learner can have access to the best of the teacher, the system has got. Also, students will have access to interacting with such excellent teachers. Further, because of digital recording and possibility of retrieval, such lessons can be revisited again for reinforcement. This process will naturally enhance the quality of learning.

Will EDUSAT Replace Teachers?

No. Never. Nothing can replace the teacher, leave alone a technology network. Such virtual classrooms involving best of the teachers will provide much needed additional support and reinforcement and the teaching and learning processes in the schools, colleges and universities for improving the quality of education. However, the effectiveness of the virtual classroom will depend very largely upon the role played by the teachers in the classrooms.

For effective learning through virtual classrooms, the teachers in the teaching end and at the reception end must, play the role of a team member (team teaching). The teacher at the reception end will help students in formulating questions, seeking clarifications from the virtual classroom teacher, solving problems on the spot, and also taking the lessons further where virtual classroom teacher concludes.

Eventually, this may help million of teachers improve their own teaching.

Is any good teacher in the classroom good enough to be the teacher in the virtual classroom?

Both 'yes' and 'no'. Yes, because he or she has the potentiality to become a good virtual classroom teacher. No, because just being a good teacher in a conventional classroom is not enough to be an effective teacher in a virtual classroom; it requires a few more additional skills over and above the knowledge of the subject and ability to communicate in a face to face situation. Conventional classroom consists of largely monologues of teachers where students remain passive listeners. This is detrimental to achieving higher levels of cognition by the students. Interactive learning is a necessary condition for achieving higher order cognition like application, analysis, synthesis, creativity, etc. One of the important, rather necessary skills of a virtual classroom teacher is to encourage students to raise their doubts, seek clarifications, make observation and generates an interactive environment. Associated skill is to manage virtual classrooms that often have 400 to 500 students - staggering and choosing questions to repond, using generic reinforcements, etc.

Ability to use audiovisual aids is an important skill for the virtual classroom teachers. Unlike the conventional television broadcast or conventional classroom of chalk and talk, the teachers will have to use a variety of educational software to make virtual classrooms interesting and effective. Besides the conventional aids like charts models, experimental demonstrations, teachers will also require electronic aids like Power point presentation, computer animation, graphics, flash, etc. Depending upon the nature of the subject and the theme, teacher may also use a fully developed interactive CD followed by discussion with the learners at distant locations.

In EDUSAT, students can ask questions during the virtual class; it is also possible to post the questions onto the web site or sent by e-mail which the teacher can respond at his or her convenience. Thus EDUSAT provides both time synchronous and asynchronous interaction.

What about the software?

Conventional software is required for conventional broadcasting. Software inventories have been developed separately for higher education, secondary and primary education. There are several thousand software titles at each level, though all of them are not of high quality. Such software has been produced by private agencies as well as state sponsored institutions.

EDUSAT professes teacher-based virtual classrooms. In this virtual classroom mode, teacher will require 'teacher support materials like charts, models, power point presentations, OHP slides, computer animation, graphics, flash, video clippings, etc. Such teacher support materials have to be prepared after content analysis of each topic to be taught through virtual classroom mode.

What will it cost? And who would provide the funds?

Satellite has been launched by the Indian Space Research Organisation (ISRO). The satellite has been offered free for education. Each uplink facility, proposed for the states and the national centres will cost approximately Rs 60 lakhs. This will be provided by the Government of India.

Each reception centres will cost approximately Rs 2.00 lakhs. This can be provided by the government depending upon the availability of funds. Since the amount required is not very high, many of the institutions like the privates schools, colleges and universities may be able to mobilise their own resources for installing the facilities. Funds can be mobilised from the alumni, from the MP and MLA funds; though not very common, there are instances where funds have been generated by the students and teachers of the colleges for bringing technology support to education.

What is the current plan?

EDUSAT will cover all kinds of learners, both within and outside the educational institutions like, women, working children and youth, etc. and in phases. Initially, it may cover primary and elementary school teachers since it will not be possible to extend the reception facilities to the primary and elementary schools directly. In higher education, lessons can be delivered directly to the students since colleges and universities can afford the reception facilities in their respective institutions. There is a proposal to provide reception facilities to the senior secondary schools in the first phase, subject to the availability of funds. To begin with, reception network will be established in the private schools at their own cost and the schools in the central sectors, namely KVS and NVS and CTSE, numbering about 10,000 that have the necessary resources. They will be encouraged to adopt two or more state board schools in the form of a complex. This network of 10,000 schools can reach out to another 20, 000 to 30,000 schools. At this level again, the lessons are to be delivered directly to the students.

The immediate decision is to equip all the District Institutes of Education and Training with the reception facilities generating a national network with the uplink facilities at IGNOU and another being set up in the NCERT. Uplink stations will be set up in 17 major states. The DIET facilities linked to the state uplink stations will generate the state-level network where teaching-learning can be conducted in the local language.

When will the EDUSAT programme be actually launched?

Well, there is no formal or final decision, yet. Certain ground level preparations can begin only after the satellite has been launched successfully and stationed in the geosynchronous orbit. It has now happened. Accordingly the procedure for purchase and installation of the ground reception facilities have begun; hopefully, it should be ready by the end of the current year (2004). And, the first programme on EDUSAT was to begin on 1st January, 2005'.*

How do you know whether EDUSAT will work? Is there any experience?

Yes, there is rich Indian experience to provide confidence that this will work. With the leftover life of INSAT, Development and Educational Communication Unit (DECU) of ISRO was encouraged to experiment with tele-education primarily through one-way video and two-way audio. One of the portable uplink stations was parked at IGNOU which developed reception network at its own regional offices. A large number of national institutions like NIEPA, NCERT, NIOS, IIT, and AIMA, other than IGNOU itself, has been successfully using the virtual classroom mode for training for several years now. There have been several occasions when DECU and IGNOU have conducted two-way videoconferencing between these two centers for training senior officials.

Two-way video interactive facilities are also there at National Informatics Centre, BHEL, BEL, ISRO. Many of these organisations use videoconferencing for executive meetings and solving problems, over and above the capability building of its staff.

---

* This was planned originally. By end of November 2005, EDUSAT programmes, except in ISRO sponsored pilot experiments have not begin.

There are several states that made pioneering efforts and generated rich experience of using virtual classrooms for capacity building. Andhra Pradesh, Karnataka, Madhya Pradesh, Orissa, Gujarat, Goa are pioneers in setting up their own interactive network at their own cost. Few other states have a reception network but not the uplink facilities. Maharashtra uses uplink facilities of Gujarat. All these have generated rich experience providing confidence that two-way video interactive channel will work to provide substantial succor in quality improvement in education.

ISRO has sponsored a number of pilot experimental projects in different locations in the country like YCMOU in Maharashtra, VTU, etc. with the support of the existing satellites. These are also generating the required experience.

How would EDUSAT be managed?

The concept document as well as the project report recommended setting up an authority at the national level for managing EDUSAT; similar structure is to be set up at the state level. Till such time the EDUSAT authority comes into being, IGNOU will act as the coordinating agency in collaboration with other major national institutions. Also, there is a core group set up by Government of India to carry out the day-to-day coordination and management.